Switzerland is universally respected for its highly successful economy – not simply its banks and cuckoo clocks, but its precision engineering, pharmaceuticals, and manufactured food industries. It has long enjoyed low unemployment, and an exceptionally successful transition process for youngsters from school to work.

This book provides a 'nuts-and-bolts' comparison with Britain of how that more successful transition is brought about. It explains the different emphases of Swiss secondary schooling: more time on mathematics and, within mathematics, more on arithmetic; in science lessons, less time on pupils' individual experimentation and more on documentation by the teacher of central scientific laws; in lessons on technology and practical subjects, less time on pupils' individual creations and more on class-wide specified tasks – whether in woodwork or domestic science – aimed at high standards of finish. Career guidance at school including periods of work experience with potential employers who provide apprenticeships (in contrast to current British policy, where spells of work experience are deliberately *not* with potential employers). Apprenticeships are undertaken in Switzerland by three quarters of all school leavers, and are completed with external practical and written tests.

A final chapter discusses current developments and lessons for Britain.

THE NATIONAL INSTITUTE OF

ECONOMIC AND SOCIAL RESEARCH

Economic and Social Studies

XXXVII

FROM SCHOOL TO

PRODUCTIVE WORK: BRITAIN AND

SWITZERLAND COMPARED

FROM SCHOOL TO PRODUCTIVE WORK
Britain and Switzerland compared

by

HELVIA BIERHOFF

and

S. J. PRAIS

CAMBRIDGE
UNIVERSITY PRESS

PUBLISHED BY THE PRESS SYNDICATE OF THE UNIVERSITY OF CAMBRIDGE
The Pitt Building, Trumpington Street, Cambridge CB2 1RP, United Kingdom

CAMBRIDGE UNIVERSITY PRESS
The Edinburgh Building, Cambridge, CB2 2RU, United Kingdom
40 West 20th Street, New York, NY 10011-4211, USA
10 Stamford Road, Oakleigh, Melbourne 3166, Australia

First published 1997

Printed in Great Britain at the University Press, Cambridge

A catalogue record for this book is available from the British Library

Catalogue record for this book is available from the Library of Congress

ISBN 0 521 59079 5 hardback
ISBN 0 521 59919 9 paperback

Contents

Figures and tables

Preface

The importance of the contrast between Britain and many Continental countries in the ways young people are educated and move on to their careers is now widely recognised. That contrast manifests itself most clearly in the role of vocational education and training and its certification, as well as in the balance of the school curriculum before sixteen. Among Continental countries in which vocational education and training are much more important than in Britain are Austria, Germany, the Netherlands and Switzerland. On the other hand, Britain now places more reliance on longer full-time education, rather than on a period of 'interleaved' work-based training and part-time college attendance for 16–20-year-olds that forms the overriding and essential element of the Continental transition from school to work. Lower youth unemployment rates, and greater motivation at secondary schools, are important accompaniments to the approach of those Continental countries relying on apprenticeship methods of vocational training.

A summary view of differences in *Productivity, Education and Training* between Britain and a number of Continental countries, based on the Institute's earlier researches, was attempted in a short book issued last year under that title. The present book can be seen as a sequel in that it points a microscope at the most economically successful of those countries, Switzerland, with a view to comparing with Britain in considerable practical detail:

—   what goes on in their secondary schools to enable a much greater proportion of school-leavers to attain high standards in core subjects;
—   how vocational guidance at school is more effective in encouraging the overwhelming majority of school-leavers to embark voluntarily on apprenticeships;
—   the mechanisms which ensure that high standards are attained at the end of a certificated apprenticeship.

In writing this book we have primarily had in mind the needs of that broad spectrum of English readers who have become concerned with re-forming English schooling and vocational training. We hope this book will help show that a better understanding of the practical details of Continental systems will lead to better policies at home, and to policies more in tune with the Continent – notwithstanding that Switzerland voted not to join the European Union. As will be seen, both our National Curriculum for those at school aged 5–16 (despite successive revisions) and qualifications for 16–19-year-olds (the subject of a further recent review by Sir Ron Dearing for the Schools Curriculum and Assessment Authority, March 1996) remain substantially out of line with Continental practice. Had we been writing primarily for Swiss readers, the balance of space in this book might have been different; for example, we might have given more attention to their current discussions on improving their schooling organisation (though something is offered here in Appendix D) and their teaching methods, and to what they might learn with advantage from the roles in England of external school examinations at age 16, and of voluntary-aided schools in providing public finance for a greater variety of schools. But our concern has been not to obscure an overall view of the major differences between the countries; we have therefore also not gone deeply into debates that are more of internal concern. The present book can serve no more than as an introduction and motivator: we have no doubt that there is scope for more extensive detailed comparative research that might fill a series of volumes.

In carrying out our researches we have been encouraged and helped by many in the world of education and industry. In England we have benefited from particularly close cooperation with the principal and senior inspectors of schools in the London Borough of Barking and Dagenham, and with teachers in that Borough. In Switzerland, we found a welcoming hand wherever we turned; in particular, the Zürich educational authorities and their schools were most generous in placing their advice and facilities at our disposal, and in sparing time for cross-visits to schools in England to help arrive at our conclusions. In addition, the kind help of Swiss federal educational institutions, and of the educational authorities and schools in Aargau, Berne and St Gallen, must be mentioned here, together with the many industrial firms which we were permitted to visit and to have detailed discussions with their vocational training departments.

Many specialists have contributed to the improvement of individual chapters; an earlier draft of the whole book benefited from detailed comments by Professor H.J. Streiff (till recently, director of the seminary for the training of teachers for *Oberschulen* and *Realschulen* in Zürich) who had inspected schools in London as part of the present research project, Dr H. Hollenstein (Deputy Director of the Centre for Research of Economic Activity at the Swiss Federal Institute of Technology in Zürich) who had previously spent a year with us at the National Institute on associated research, Mr R. Bernheim (for many decades, London correspondent of the *Neue Zürischer Zeitung*) and an anonymous referee. Frau Trudi Sprock allowed us to include in Appendix C a translated version of an article by her on the socialisation of pupils in Swiss secondary schools. We are indebted to them all, as to colleagues in our team at the Institute – Geoff Mason, Valerie Jarvis and Julia Whitburn – and to the Institute's Director, Martin Weale, for general advice, encouragement, and detailed improvements. Needless to say, remaining errors of fact or judgement must be blamed solely on the authors.

The Institute is glad to acknowledge the generous financial support for this research provided by the Leverhulme Foundation and by the Gatsby Charitable Foundation.

H.B., S.J.P.
London
April 1996

1   Two very different educational ideals

This is a book about everyday life in Britain and Switzerland – how young people go to school, what they learn, how they choose their careers, and how they train to produce goods and services that are in international demand and earn high incomes. Outstandingly marvellous as Britain's contribution was in leading the industrial revolution and in serving as a beacon of democracy, doubts have increased as to whether its education and training systems are now all that they should be in an increasingly technological and developing world. Questions are increasingly asked whether in other countries education and training taken as a whole are substantially better than here; and, if so, what are the precise and substantial aspects in which they differ; and whether Britain's problems – insofar as they lie in the fields of education and training – could be solved simply by 'more money'.

To help cast light on these issues, an unusually close inquiry into another country's educational and training arrangements was undertaken by the National Institute: it was 'unusual' in that it relied not, as often in social and economic research, simply on consideration of statistics and learned articles plus short site-visits by the investigators, but was substantially based on the expert judgement of teams of experienced practitioners – teachers, inspectors, vocational experts – who took part in a structured series of visits to educational institutions and employers' training establishments in Switzerland, together with return visits to Britain by Swiss experts.

But why, the reader will ask, choose Switzerland for such an investigation rather than, say, deepening our researches into the German system, or the United States, France or Japan? Indeed, why go abroad at all when much might be learnt within Britain itself by comparing good schools and good training-employers with those of only average performance or below?

Some brief answers to these questions may be attempted at the outset, though a full justification can appear only in the course of ensuing chapters as we compare details and analyse the issues at stake. Let us begin with the limitations of comparisons solely within Britain. First, there are the disadvantages of insularity – of comparing only variants that have become accepted in Britain, rather than the wider range of possibilities opened by a critical examination of arrangements in other countries. Secondly, in whatever way samples of (say) schools are chosen within Britain for comparative evaluation, those schools that are exemplary will include an undue proportion with children from homes that attach importance to study; as a result, such schools attract good teachers, have better organised lessons with less indiscipline, have good final examination results, attract more families of that sort to the area, and so cumulatively reinforce that process. The obverse for unsatisfactory schools need not be spelled out. Comparisons *within* Britain may well help in deepening our understanding of these mutually reinforcing cumulative processes, and our understanding of the difficulties in changing them: they cannot provide much guidance for the average teacher who is keen to raise the school-leaving attainments of an average mix of pupils to the standards attained by their counterparts abroad.

Looking for inspiration to the United States is no longer as attractive as it used to be; its 'blackboard jungle', the low attainments of its average secondary school pupils in international tests, heavy youth unemployment, later age of university graduation than in Britain – these are well-known limitations of its highly expensive system of education. Americans now look increasingly to Continental Europe for features of its apprenticeship system which might be grafted onto its own post-compulsory schooling framework, and so help raise the capabilities of its lower-attaining school-leavers. If we turn to Japan, it is undisputed that its industrial efficiency and the extraordinarily high attainments of its school-leavers provide great challenges to western thinking: yet a great cultural gap makes one hesitate in drawing immediately applicable policy conclusions. Japanese home life in general, and the mother in particular, place greater emphasis on supporting and furthering a child's schooling attainments; and the balance of ultimate objectives in a Japanese child's upbringing is very different from that desired in Britain – conformity is given much greater emphasis than individuality, and extending the child's span of attention and concentration is valued more than the spontaneity and creativity which have become the shibboleths of English progressive educationists.

Switzerland's achievements

The greater cultural similarity between Britain and its Continental neighbours suggests that relevant policy lessons would be drawn more readily from nearer home; we need to look more closely at the Continent before going further afield. France and Germany have been the subject of a number of comparisons (by the National Institute as well as by many others) and provided much support for the view that higher attainments in Britain are both possible and necessary in schooling, training and productivity. Deeper investigations are however necessary to understand by what specific methods Continental schooling arrangements promote the higher attainments of their school-leavers, how vocational guidance at their schools contributes to encouraging so many more to take up skilled apprenticeships, and which features of their vocational qualification systems contribute to their attractiveness. In choosing Switzerland for the present deeper investigation, the following advantages can be listed:

(a) For an economist, its extraordinarily high real income per head – as high as the United States, 15–20 per cent above Germany and France, and 31 per cent above the UK (as estimated in the most recent purchasing-power-parity comparisons for 1990) – is sufficient for an inquiry into the qualifications of its workforce that contribute to that remarkable achievement.[1]

(b) The reputation of Swiss manufactures reinforces our interest in skill formation: Switzerland's precision engineering, industrial chemicals, pharmaceuticals, and food industries have acquired a worldwide renown for high quality. Despite Switzerland's small size – only a tenth of the UK's population – it is among the world's largest exporters of specialised high-quality manufactured goods; for example, Switzerland accounts for 45 per cent of world exports of weaving machines, 37 per cent of platen printing presses, 34 per cent of watches, 32 per cent of vegetable alkaloids and derivatives.[2] Its total exports of machine tools

---

[1] *Purchasing Power Parities and Real Expenditures, EKS Results*, vol. 1, OECD 1992, pp. 28–9. A recent inquiry at the National Institute by Valerie Jarvis and S.J. Prais suggested that the gaps in real incomes between Britain and Germany (and, by implication, Switzerland) are likely to be considerably greater than indicated by those estimates because of inadequate allowance in the underlying PPP comparisons for quality differences in the products produced in the various countries (The quality of manufactured products in Britain and Germany, *National Institute Discussion Paper* no. 88, December 1995).

[2] S. Borner, N.E. Porter, R. Weder and M. Enwright, *Internationale Wettbewerbsvorteile: Ein strategisches Konzept für die Schweiz* (Campus, Frankfurt, 1991), p. 103.

are the third largest in the world, after Germany and Japan, and double those of the UK; expressed per head of each country's workforce in the whole economy, Switzerland's exports of machine tools in 1992 were double Germany's, seven times Japan's, and fifteen times the UK's.

(c) Switzerland has been more successful in avoiding the problems of youth unemployment that have increasingly plagued Britain in the past decade; unemployment among Swiss young people aged under 25 in 1992 was only 5 per cent of the labour force in that age group, compared with 15 per cent in the UK, 21 per cent in France and 6 per cent in Germany.[3] The Swiss system of vocational training for school-leavers resembles Germany's in many respects (yet with significant differences, as explained in Chapter 4), and the detailed 'mechanics' of its vocational guidance and training systems are worth careful study in relation to recent and planned changes in Britain.

(d) Switzerland's mountainous terrain provides extraordinary natural *disad*vantages to transport, travel and communications; there are no 'great central plains' on which crops can be grown efficiently; and no natural resources to speak of (in contrast to Germany's coal and iron).[4] True, its mountains were among the factors protecting it against the ravages of two World Wars; that factor undoubtedly contributed to its rapid economic development in earlier decades, but can hardly be a significant continuing element in today's increasingly global economy. The nature of its workforce skills, and the institutional arrangements for developing those skills, thus invited detailed investigation.

(e) Since the times of the Swiss educationist Pestalozzi (1746–1827) – widely regarded (especially, of course, in Switzerland!) as one of the great founders of modern universal education – it has been a particular objective of Swiss schooling to develop an appropriate combination of *intellectual* and *practical* aspects of schooling: it is clearly worth exploring the con-

---

[3] *The OECD Jobs Study* (Paris, 1994), Part 1, p. 43. Movements of migrant workers have often contributed to cushioning unemployment in Switzerland. Whatever contribution that factor may have made in the past, the current situation is that the children of migrants form an unusually large proportion of school pupils (of the order of a fifth in Zürich in 1995), and the additional provisions made for their difficulties seem adequate to ensure that they find apprenticeship places and subsequent employment.

[4] Borner *et al.*, p. 212.

trasts with Britain, where intellectual elements have often been regarded as more important.

Opportunities and pressures to assess the relative advantages of neighbouring countries' education and training systems in practical detail are particularly open in Switzerland because of its extensive borders and linguistic plurality; in addition, Switzerland has the distinction of being governed in a highly participative and decentralised way. There are consequent differences within Switzerland in respect of schooling and training which express themselves in variations at Cantonal levels in legislation on curricula, examinations and related organisational and financial responsibilities. The present study has taken for its focus the German-speaking part of Switzerland, within which variations are smaller; it is the largest sector, with 74 per cent of all Swiss nationals and 65 per cent of all its inhabitants having German as their mother tongue. To have ventured more widely into French and Italian parts of the country would have led to undue dissipation of our research resources – and to wearying detail in the present report.[5]

Qualifications of the workforce

The distinction of Switzerland's training and education systems is at once evident on comparing the qualifications attained by its workforce with the UK. Household sample interview surveys, which include questions on vocational and educational qualifications of all living at each sampled address, are now carried out routinely in both countries (in Switzerland, only since 1991) on more or less common principles and provide an adequate basis for such comparisons; summary results for the two countries are shown in table 1.1, together with those for Germany – a touchstone in these matters. Five broad levels of qualification – from university level to those

---

[5] French and Italian parts of Switzerland rely to a greater extent on full-time college-based vocational education (as in their neighbouring countries) rather than on apprenticeship combined with part-time college education as in the German-speaking parts. At the same time, it is a matter of concern that youth unemployment is higher in the French and Italian parts than in the German-speaking parts. For statistics on languages, see *Statistisches Jahrbuch der Schweiz*, 1992, p. 323.

Table 1.1   *Highest vocational qualifications attained by the labour force[a] in Britain (1990), Switzerland (1991) and Germany (1991)*

	Britain	Switzerland	Germany[b]
Degree level[c]	11	10	10
Higher intermediate (technician)[d]	7	12	8
Lower intermediate (craft)[e]	9	55	54
Basic vocational qualifications[f]	8	2	
No vocational qualifications, but general educational qualifi-cations which are:			
high or medium[g]	30	2	n.a.
low or none[h]	<u>35</u>	<u>19</u>	<u>n.a.</u>
	<u>65</u>	<u>21</u>	<u>28</u>
	100	100	100

Sources:
Britain: Based on Labour Force Survey 1990, *Employment Gazette*, March 1992, and estimated mapping of NVQ levels in *Employment Gazette*, July 1992, p. 346; and special tabulations. *Switzerland*: Based on *Die Schweizerische Arbeitskräfteerhebung (SAKE)*, Bundesamt für Statistik, Bern, 1992; and special tabulations. Germany: *Fachserie 1 Reihe 4.1.2: Beruf, Ausbildung und Arbeitsbedingungen der Erwerbstätigen 1991*, Statistisches Bundesamt, Wiesbaden.

Notes:

[a]Per cent of persons in employment. For Britain, persons of working age (men aged 16–64, women aged 16–59) in employment.

[b]German figures are presented here for approximate comparison only; respondents not providing information on vocational qualifications were classified in the original sources together with those without a vocational qualification.

[c]For Britain: first and higher degrees and equivalent (for example, graduate membership of professional institutes). For Switzerland: university degrees, *Höhere Fachschule* qualifications, extra-university qualifications of an equivalent level including those teaching qualifications regarded by the Swiss as being of an equivalent level.

[d]For Britain: BTEC HNC/D, nursing qualifications, non-graduate teachers. For Switzerland: *Technikerschule* and *Meister* qualifications, some non-graduate teachers (estimated from those classified under *Matura* in the Swiss LFS; the latter group includes primary school teachers as well as persons with only general educational qualifications).

[e]For Britain: City and Guilds parts II and III (estimated at 20 per cent of all City and Guilds qualifications in the LFS, on the basis of *Employment Gazette*, July 1992),

Notes to table continued

BTEC National qualifications (estimated at 70 per cent of the published combined figure for BTEC General/First and National qualifications, on the basis of *Employment Gazette*); half of trade apprenticeships (on the basis of *Employment Gazette*). For Switzerland: apprenticeships, full-time vocational colleges; the figure includes an estimated three quarters of those classified under *Diplommittelschule* and an estimated 35 per cent of those classified under *Matura* (see text fn. 6).

[f]For Britain: City and Guilds part I (estimated at 40 per cent of all responding to the LFS as having City and Guilds qualifications); 15 per cent of BTEC General/First and National qualifications; half of trade apprenticeships (see note c). YTS trainees are not included unless they have also attained a vocational qualification. For Switzerland: half of all responding to the LFS as having obtained *Anlehre* qualifications (the *Berufsbildungsgesetz* of 1980 requirestraining and course attendance, but does not specify examined standards for the award of this qualification; half have therefore here been treated as not attaining a basic vocational qualification).

[g]For Britain: GCE A-levels and O-levels or equivalent, and 20 per cent of all City and Guilds qualifications to represent those who have obtained qualifications below NVQ level 2. For Switzerland: three quarters of *Matura* and *Diplommittelschule* qualifications. The figures for Switzerland incorporate estimates (see text fn. 6).

[h]For Britain: CSEs below grade 1, 20 per cent of City and Guilds qualifications, 15 per cent of BTEC General/First and National qualifications, and those recorded as having no qualifications. For Switzerland: no qualifications (2 per cent), those completing *obligatorische Grundschule*, and half of those classified under *Anlehre* (see note d). The figures also include young people who are in vocational training and have not yet completed it.

who are virtually unqualified – are distinguished here, as follows (details of constituent qualifications, and definitional adjustments for international comparability, are in footnotes to the table and below)[6]:

(a) *Degree-level qualifications* First and higher university degrees or equivalent qualifications, for example, graduate membership of professional institutes in Britain, Federal Polytechnics (*Eidgnössische Technische Hochschule*) in Switzerland.

(b) *Higher-intermediate (technician-level) qualifications* Qualifications below degree level but above craft level; for example, BTEC Higher Cer-

---

[6] Some elements of approximation and estimation have been necessary for the sake of international comparability, but they are unlikely to affect our central conclusions in any substantial way; the general problems in comparing the two countries' Labour Force Surveys are noted here, while detailed points are recorded in footnotes to the table. For both countries these surveys give the *highest* qualification obtained by each person questioned, based on a conventionally defined ranking; but the ranking conventions unfortunately differ between the two countries, and we have therefore been obliged to introduce indirect and rough estimates to establish definitional comparability. The highest qualification can be either a *vocational* qualification or a *general educational* qualification: if someone has both types, and his general educational qualification is ranked above his vocational qualification, then the vocational qualification is not recorded in the LFS. Because of our concern here with economic performance, where a person has both vocational and educational qualifications, he has been reclassified by his vocational qualification, sometimes using informal estimates. For example, on the basis of discussions in Switzerland, we allocated three quarters of those recorded there as having as their highest qualification a high or intermediate general educational qualification as also having acquired a vocational qualification. A further problem attaches to the Swiss LFS category *Matura*, which comprises both general educational qualifications equivalent to English A-levels and certain primary school teaching qualifications; we assumed that three quarters of those classified under *Matura* have also obtained a vocational qualification, though that may be an underestimate. In the latest (but varying in earlier) British LFS, all general educational qualifications below higher education level are ranked below vocational qualifications; the difficulties just described do not therefore arise when considering the latest British LFS. Important problems in interpreting the British LFS arose where very different levels of qualification were recorded as belonging to the same category; for example, no distinction was made between parts I, II or III of City and Guilds qualifications, or between BTEC First/General and National qualifications. In such cases we applied the mapping of LFS data to NVQ levels given in the *Employment Gazette*, July 1992, p. 346.

tificates and Diplomas in Britain, *Höhere Fachschulen* and *Ingenieurschulen* qualifications in Switzerland.

(c) *Lower-intermediate (craft-level) qualifications* For example, in Britain, City and Guilds parts II and III, BTEC National qualifications; in Switzerland, qualifications certifying examined completion of apprenticeship-type training courses lasting 2–4 years.

(d) *Basic vocational qualifications* Vocational qualifications below craft level; for example, in Britain, City and Guilds part I; in Switzerland, basic traineeships (*Anlehre*) generally of only one year's duration.

(e) *No vocational qualifications* Those with no *vocational* qualifications, of whom some may have general educational qualifications. We have here sub-divided general educational qualifications into (i) a higher and medium category, corresponding to A-levels or 'higher grades' GCSE (A–C) in England, and *Matura* in Switzerland; and (ii) a lower category – those with lower GCSE grades (below C) or no general educational qualifications, and completion of *Volkschule* in Switzerland.

It will not be forgotten, of course, that these categories represent simplifications of an underlying more continuous and more complex reality, and also that many individuals may have acquired skills without having acquired formal qualifications. Nevertheless, three important contrasts between Britain and Switzerland can be drawn from this table with reasonable confidence. First, there is virtually no difference between the two countries in the proportions having attained university-level qualifications: 11 per cent of the working population in Britain, 10 per cent in Switzerland. Secondly, there appear to be extraordinarily large differences between the proportions with intermediate vocational qualifications: 67 per cent hold intermediate qualifications in Switzerland – taking technician and craft qualifications together – as against 16 per cent in Britain. There is less difference at the technician, higher-intermediate, level (at 12 compared with 7 per cent of the workforce); the bulk of the difference is at the craft, or lower-intermediate, level, where 55 per cent hold such qualifications in Switzerland as against only 9 per cent in Britain. Whatever might be thought about the proportion of the British workforce which had acquired skills without accompanying paper qualifications, it seems unrealistic to suppose that this bridges more than a small fraction of the gap. Thirdly, comparison of the proportions with only basic vocational qualifications, or no qualifications, yields naturally the converse: only about 20 per cent of the labour force in Switzerland are at this level, compared with roughly 65 per cent in Britain. A summary way of putting these comparisons is to note that about *three quarters of the Swiss workforce is vocationally qualified to levels reached only by the top quarter of the British workforce.*[7]

Comparison with Germany (final column of table 1.1) indicates that Switzerland has a workforce qualification structure fairly similar to Germany's. But there is also a suggestion that Switzerland is at a slight advantage in some respects: while closely similar proportions have qualified to university level, a greater proportion has qualified to higher-

---

[7] Official sources in the UK from time to time fall prey to the temptation to convey a more flattering picture of its workforce qualifications, which is radically misleading when set in international context. For example, the Department of Employment's *Labour Market Quarterly Report* (February 1993) said: 'Almost three out of every four people of working age in Great Britain have a qualification. ... Over half are qualified to A level or above.' A hurried reader could easily understand this to mean that over half of all persons of working age in Britain are qualified to A-level or above. But the text was 'badly written' (as an official at the Department of Employment explained in response to our request for elucidation); the second sentence should read: 'Over half [of the three quarters of persons of working age who have a qualification] are qualified to A level or above', *that is,* the proportion of such people out of *all* people of working age is under, rather than over, a half. But even that is subject to reservations. First, time-served apprenticeships were treated as of A-level standard; however, the assumption that all who have served such an apprenticeship are educated to the same level as those who have passed A-level examinations is grossly over-optimistic, since time-serving does not require part-time college attendance nor a final examination. Secondly, City and Guilds certificates, and BTEC/BEC/TEC qualifications below Higher level, were all classified as equivalent to A-level standard. This, again, is a gross oversimplification since no distinction was made between the three levels of City and Guilds passes (the lowest of which is only of about secondary school leaving standard), and between the two levels of BTEC/BEC/TEC qualifications below Higher level. Other estimates by the Employment Department, BTEC, and City and Guilds (see fn. 6 above) indicate that 80 per cent of City and Guilds passes, and 30 per cent of BTEC qualifications below Higher level, are below NVQ level 3 (that is, below craft level). Putting all these qualifications on a par with qualifications entitling the holder to university entrance suggests, shall we say, some lack of touch with reality. Discounting these groups radically reduces the proportion of people that can be considered as educated to A-level or above. An official interpretation of the available British surveys, broadly consistent with the text above, has now been provided in *Education Statistics for the United Kingdom: 1995 Edition* (HMSO, 1996), table 36 (b).

Table 1.2 *Qualifications of the labour force in Britain (1990) and Switzerland (1991) in manufacturing and non-manufacturing*

	Manufacturing		Non-manufacturing	
	Switzerland	Britain	Switzerland	Britain
Degree level	7	7	11	12
Higher intermediate (technician)	9	5	13	8
Lower intermediate (craft)	<u>57</u>	<u>12</u>	<u>54</u>	<u>8</u>
	66	17	67	16
Basic vocational qualifications	3	11	2	7
No vocational qualifications, but general educational qualifications which are:				
high or medium	2	23	3	32
low or none	24	42	17	32
	<u>25</u>	<u>65</u>	<u>20</u>	<u>64</u>
	100	100	100	100

Sources: See table 1.1.
Notes: See notes to table 1.1. The numbers in the category *Matura* in the Swiss LFS have been allocated differentially here to take account of primary school teachers who are almost entirely in non-manufacturing (see text fn. 4 and notes b, c and e of table 1.1), as follows. In non-manufacturing, half of those classified under *Matura* in the LFS are have been allocated to 'higher intermediate' to allow for primary school teachers; one quarter to 'lower intermediate', as likely to have obtained a vocational qualification at craft level; and the remaining quarter to 'high or medium general educational qualifications'. In manufacturing, three quarters of those classified under *Matura* in the LFS are included in 'lower intermediate', the remainder in 'high or medium general educational qualifications'.

intermediate level in Switzerland than in Germany (at 12 compared with 8 per cent).[8] Similarly, taking all intermediate qualifications together – higher, lower and basic – Switzerland appears to have 69 per cent of its workforce so qualified compared with 62 per cent in Germany. The proportion in Switzerland without any vocational qualifications is, correspondingly, slightly lower than in Germany, at about 21 per cent in Switzerland compared with 28 per cent in Germany; both these countries

[8] This is partly (but only partly) because seminary-trained teachers in Switzerland are classified at sub-graduate level (non-graduates' routes to teaching were abolished in Germany during the 1970s, and the German microcensus now classifies all teachers as being of 'university level').

stand in considerable contrast to Britain where that proportion is 64 per cent, that is, about two or three times as high.

In short, we see that Britain's deficiencies in qualified personnel do not arise at the most highly qualified 10–15 per cent slice of the workforce but – as appeared also from the Institute's previous comparisons with France and the Netherlands – at the intermediate level of vocational qualifications. It is arguable that the relatively large proportion of young people in Britain who have obtained higher or medium general educational qualifications, even though they have no vocational qualifications, have more *potential* for acquiring vocational skills than those who have not done so; and they might therefore be classified in a higher category than we have done here. However, as is widely accepted in Switzerland, *general educational qualifications are by no means an adequate substitute for the practical skills and specialised theoretical knowledge* relevant to a particular occupation that young people acquire through a training programme leading to a recognised vocational qualification (obtained typically in Switzerland, as detailed in chapter 4, after 2–4 years of vocational training with accompanying part-time attendance at a vocational college). To regard these two types of qualification as substitutes obscures vital differences between the qualification structures and workforce capabilities of the two countries.

The above pattern for the workforce as a whole is evident almost equally in manufacturing and non-manufacturing considered separately, as shown in table 1.2. In both countries the proportions qualified to university degree level are much the same: 7 per cent in manufacturing, and 11–12 per cent in non-manufacturing: more university graduates are found in non-manufacturing, since that sector includes professional occupations (lawyers, accountants, and so on). At craft level, Britain's relative shortfall of qualified persons is slightly lower in manufacturing than in non-manufacturing, in that Switzerland has five times more persons qualified to this level than Britain in manufacturing, and six and a half times as many in non-manufacturing. On the other hand, at technician level Britain's relative shortfall appears greater in manufacturing than in non-manufacturing, though the absolute gap is only 4–5 per cent of the workforce. These differences between craft and technician levels reflect mainly the relatively greater role in Britain of apprenticeships in manufacturing, and the relative paucity of systematic schemes of training outside manufacturing.[9]

---

[9] Figures in table 1.2 are shown to the nearest 1 per cent; the original computations for higher-intermediate level, rounded to two significant digits for comparisons of ratios, were as follows (they should not be treated too precisely): in manufac-

Table 1.3 *Percentage of all 19-year-olds passing vocational examinations at craft level in five selected occupational groups in Britain (1989), Switzerland (1991) and Germany (1991)*

Occupational group	Britain	Switzerland	Germany
Mechanical	1.5	3.7	6.3
Electrical	2.0	5.0	5.0
Construction	2.2	5.2	4.5
Office work	3.2	21.8	19.3
Retailing	0.2	6.3	7.2
	9.1	42.0	42.3

Sources: Britain: City and Guilds, *Examination Statistics,* 1988–89 (Part II or equivalent), BTEC *Annual Report and Examination Statistics,* 1989 (mimeo; National Certificate and Diploma). Switzerland: Bundesamt für Statistik, *Statistik der Lehrabschlussprüfungen und Lehrverträge 1991* (mimeo). Germany: Statistisches Bundesamt, *Bildung und Kultur: Berufliche Bildung,* 1991; *Berufliche Schulen,* 1991.

Note: For details of occupational groups, see Appendix A. Figures available for Britain for years after 1989 are difficult to interpret following the reorganisation of qualifications consequent on the introduction of NVQs (see Appendix B).

Recent trends in more detail

To examine recent trends in the rate of qualification in greater occupational detail, and to help judge whether the gaps between the countries are likely to decrease, we must next examine recent *flows* of qualifications (as distinct from the comparisons so far of *stocks* of qualified manpower). We shall discuss, first, flows at craft level – the level at which the greatest contrast between Britain and Switzerland has arisen in the past; and, secondly, flows at university level, where government policy in Britain has recently promoted an extraordinarily rapid expansion.

---

turing 5.3 per cent of persons in employment were qualified to higher-intermediate level in Britain, compared with 9.3 per cent in Switzerland; in non-manufacturing the proportions qualified to higher-intermediate level were 7.7 per cent in Britain and and 12.8 per cent in Switzerland. At higher-intermediate level in manufacturing, Switzerland thus has a three quarters' greater proportion than Britain, whereas in non-manufacturing Switzerland's proportion is two thirds greater.

Craft-level qualifications

At craft level we concentrate on five major occupational groups: mechanical engineering, electrical engineering, construction, office work, and retailing. The numbers qualifying per annum at the beginning of this decade in these five occupational groups accounted for 42 per cent of all 19-year-olds in both Switzerland and Germany, while in Britain only 9 per cent of the comparable age group obtained such qualifications (as shown in summary form in table 1.3; detailed occupations are shown in Appendix A). That is, some 4–5 times as great a proportion of the age group qualified each year in Switzerland and Germany as in the UK in these major occupational groups. Our previous comparisons of total *stocks* of qualified persons (table 1.1 above) showed an overall gap of 5–6-fold; there is thus little indication here of a significant prospective narrowing of the gap between Britain and these countries.

In the three 'production' occupations – mechanics, electricians and construction workers – the gap in flows is somewhat narrower, in that the proportions qualifying in Switzerland are (only!) two and a half times as high as in Britain. The gap is wider in other occupations: in office work the proportion in Switzerland obtaining commercial and clerical qualifications, at BTEC National or equivalent level, is seven times the proportion in Britain; if we include lower-level office qualifications of the kind that can be obtained after one-year courses (BTEC First level or equivalent in Britain), the gap reduces slightly to fivefold.[10] The gap is wider still in retailing, where the proportion obtaining qualifications in Britain was a mere 3–4 per cent of Switzerland's. To those more concerned with self-service supermarkets, extended courses of training in retailing may not seem very important; but that view overlooks the wider benefits of further general education, and training in general commercial skills, that are essential constituents of Swiss traineeships in retailing (further details in chapter 4).

---

[10] The details are as follows. In 1991 some 3,600 students in Switzerland obtained a qualification following a *Handelsdiplomand* course of one year's duration (based on published statistics of enrolments for this course, less an allowance for dropouts and failures estimated from the corresponding three-year course); this represents an additional 4 per cent of the age group, raising the total proportion of the age group obtaining commercial qualifications from 22 to 25 per cent. In Britain, 16,600 commercial/clerical qualifications at BTEC First level or equivalent were awarded in 1989; this represents 2 per cent of the age group, bringing the total of current commercial/clerical qualifications in Britain to 5 per cent – that is, to about a fifth of the Swiss proportion.

In comparison with Germany (final column of table 1.3), the proportions of the age group obtaining vocational qualifications in Switzerland are broadly similar in these occupational groups. But perhaps one difference between Switzerland and Germany is worth noticing: in mechanical occupations, the proportion qualifying in Germany is roughly 70 per cent higher than in Switzerland. This partly reflects the greater importance of engineering and vehicle-related industries in Germany than in Switzerland (about 4 per cent of the workforce are employed in machine and vehicle production in Switzerland, compared with 10 per cent in Germany).

Between 1978 and 1991 the proportion of 20-year-olds in Switzerland undertaking an apprenticeship increased, from 59 to 72 per cent of the age cohort. This rise was mostly attributable to a marked increase in women undertaking craft-level vocational qualifications; women were originally less qualified vocationally than men but by 1991 were well on the way to catching up (only 47 per cent of young women, compared with 71 per cent of young men, held vocational qualifications at craft level at age 20 in 1978; by 1991 the corresponding proportions were 67 and 78 per cent). During the same period the number of 20-year-olds with no post-compulsory education, or having only a very basic vocational qualification, decreased from 28 to 13 per cent of the age cohort; the relative decrease was much the same for women and men, but the proportion of women in that category in 1991 was still almost twice as high as the proportion of men.[11]

In recent years an increasing proportion of pupils leaving secondary schools at age fifteen have continued in some form of voluntary full-time general or prevocational education for a further year, rather than immediately taking up an apprenticeship. Detailed information available for Zürich indicates that the proportion of 16-year-olds who continued in full-time

---

[11] Bundesamt für Statistik, *Ausbildung der Zwanzigjährigen (Sekundarstufe II) nach Geschlecht seit 1977/78* (mimeo, May 1992); these statistics relate to apprenticeships lasting for two or more years. A long-standing trend towards increased take-up of vocational training at craft level in Switzerland is also evident from a comparison of different age groups in the population available for 1988. The proportion of those then aged 30–35 who had obtained a craft-level vocational qualification was one and a half times as high as the proportion of those aged 60–70; the increase was somewhat sharper for women than for men. Of the younger group, only some 15 per cent had no post-compulsory education, compared with 50 per cent of the older group; the decrease in the proportions with no post-compulsory education or training has been sharper for women than for men, but remained slightly higher for women (at 18 per cent) than for men (13 per cent).

general or prevocational education rose from 30 to 37 per cent between 1984 and 1991, that is, by 1 per cent of the age group each year; the rise has continued subsequently.[12] In contrast to Britain, it is of interest that this change was not simply a substitute for vocational training; rather, it seems that more 15-year-old school-leavers waited an extra year in order to be better prepared to take up a more technically demanding apprenticeship, or to wait for a vacancy for an apprenticeship in an occupation closer to their talents and interests. Since about 1992, following the widespread recession and associated employment difficulties, there has been some decline in apprenticeships even in Switzerland; it is too soon to know to what extent this represents an increased trend towards full-time education, or merely a further postponement of vocational training to a later age.

We must now consider recent changes in Britain. In our comparisons so far of the numbers of young people qualifying at craft level in a recent year (set out in table 1.3 above) we deliberately selected 1989 for Britain; the reason is that this was probably the latest year before the great reforms of vocational qualifications introduced by the National Council for Vocational Qualifications – established in 1986 – affected the situation. The changes introduced by NCVQ were revolutionary in many respects – in scope of skills and theoretical understanding required, methods of assessing candidates, and compilation of statistics on the number of persons qualifying. The substantial differences between Switzerland and Britain in skills covered and the ways they are tested will be discussed in chapter 4 below; here we must only notice that the number of persons recorded by NCVQ as qualifying at what can be regarded as craft level (now known as NVQ Level 3), in the five major occupations considered above, appear to amount to no more than 1–2 per cent of the age group in 1994, compared with 9 per cent for 1989 as shown in table 1.3. Possibly the true fall in skill formation has not been as great as suggested by these figures of qualifications awarded; details of these numbers are discussed in Appendix B. It is however clear that a huge gap between Britain and the Continent remains at craft level; and that NVQs have proved to be a highly disappointing initiative in many respects.[13]

---

[12] S. Stutz-Delmore, *Schul- und Berufsausbildung der Jugendlichen im Kanton Zürich*, Erziehungsdirektion des Kantons Zürich, March 1992; and *Schulstatistik* (Zürich), April 1995, p. 6.

[13] Two official inquiries into further reforms of NCVQ were published at the end of 1995: the Beaumont *Review of 100 NVQs and SVQs*, and the GNVQ *Assessment Review* by D.R. Copey; these followed other critical reports from Ofsted and FEFC. It is as yet far from obvious that satisfactory reforms will be forthcoming (see chapters 4 and 5 below).

University qualifications

It has long been taken as axiomatic in Britain that more university graduates are needed. Universities (together with the former polytechnics) in Britain have recently expanded at such a pace that numbers of students receiving first degrees more than doubled in the last 20 years: they reached 19 per cent of the age cohort in 1991, and university entrants are projected to approach 30 per cent within the next few years.[14] While expansion of university education has been a worldwide phenomenon, the proportion of the relevant age cohort attaining university qualifications in Britain in 1991 was significantly above both Germany (13 per cent) and Switzerland (11 per cent).[15] The growth pattern of British education has thus been closer to the American model in focusing on expanding upper educational levels, whereas the German–Swiss educational model has a stronger focus on deepening the attainments of average and lower-attaining school-leavers. The latter type of policy clearly has important advantages today in assisting those whose employment is in the process of being displaced by advances in automation and by increasing competition in labour-intensive products from low-wage countries.

Despite the increase in Britain in the number of university graduates there continues to be concern about the distribution of students among the main subjects of study and the relative ability levels of students. In relation to the size of the relevant age groups (see table 1.4), numbers in Britain obtaining languages and arts degrees are roughly three times as high as in Switzerland and Germany; in mathematics and pure sciences Britain is about twice as high; in engineering – where British numbers used to be

---

[14] The Confederation of British Industries speaks even of 40 per cent as an appropriate target. We here use the term 'university' to include universities and other higher-education institutions, for example, *Höhere Fachschulen* in Switzerland.

[15] The age cohort chosen for each country was based on the average age of graduation: for Britain 21–22, for Switzerland and Germany 27. The OECD report on education in Switzerland under-reported Swiss tertiary education (*Reviews of National Policies for Education: Switzerland*, OECD, 1991, pp. 31, 34, table 6); it relied on too narrow a definition and excluded Swiss *Höhere Fachschulen* (and other higher-education institutions corresponding broadly to the former British polytechnics).

Table 1.4   *University students awarded first degrees or equivalent[a] in Britain (1991), Switzerland (1991) and Germany (1991) by main subject of study*

	Per cent of relevant age group[b]		
	Britain[c]	Switzerland	Germany
Languages and arts[d]	3.0	1.0	1.2
Social studies	1.9	1.1	1.1
Teaching[e]	1.5	1.5	0.9
Vocational Studies[f]	3.9	3.6	4.2
Maths and Science	3.2	1.3	1.5
Medicine	1.2	0.9	1.2
Engineering	2.1	2.2	2.6
Other[g]	2.6	0.0	0.1
	19.3	11.4	12.8

Sources: Britain: based on *Education Statistics for the United Kingdom: 1994 Edition*, table 3.4, together with information on PGCE and subject distribution from: Universities Funding Council, *University Statistics 1992–93*, vol. 2, 1994. Germany: based on Statistisches Bundesamt, *Statistisches Jahrbuch 1993*. Switzerland: based on Bundesamt für Statistik, special tabulations.
Notes: [a]For Britain: university and CNAA degrees; for Germany: university and *Fachhochschule Diplom, Staatsexamen, Magister*, and equivalent; for Switzerland: university *Lizentiate* and *Diplome*, extra-university higher-education qualifications (including *Höhere Fachschule* qualifications). Double-counting has been eliminated as far as possible, as noted in later footnotes.
[b]Relates to 27-year-olds in Germany and Switzerland (numbering 1,190,000 and 116,000 respectively), and to 21–22-year-olds in Britain (estimated at 860,000).
[c]Figures include estimates of Open University degrees (totalling 1 per cent of the age cohort), for which a subject breakdown is not available in sufficient detail.
[d]Includes 25 per cent of extra-university higher-education qualifications in theology; a 75 per cent overlap is assumed between these and university degrees in theology.
[e]For Britain: estimate based on the proportion of new graduates going on to obtain a PGCE; the British figures of graduates in the other areas of study have been reduced proportionally. For Switzerland, a 50 per cent overlap is assumed between extra-university higher-education examinations for teaching and university degrees in arts and languages and in science and mathematics.
[f]Includes economics, law, architecture, agriculture, business and administration. For Switzerland; includes in addition 25 per cent of extra-university higher-education qualifications in law (a 75 per cent overlap is estimated between these and law university degrees).
[g]For Britain: Combined and General Studies (under 11 per cent of these, i.e. under 0.2 per cent of the age group, have an engineering content). For Germany: sports.

considerably lower – Britain is now close to Switzerland, if still about a quarter lower than Germany.[16]

While places available for university engineering students have increased substantially in Britain in the past decade, there has been a worrying side-effect that entrance requirements for engineering courses have been reduced. For example, the absolute number of acceptances for university engineering courses of students who had low A-level qualifications (ten A-level points or less, that is, no more than, say, two subjects at grade D and one at grade E) increased fourfold between 1986 and 1992, from 300 a year to 1,270.[17] Conversely, it became more difficult to attract high-calibre students to engineering courses at universities: despite the great increase in the total number of university entrants, the absolute number of acceptances to engineering and technology courses of high-calibre students, those with 26 A-level points or more (say, those who passed three subjects with at least two Bs and one A, or equivalent), *fell* by about a tenth (from 3,530 to 3,240) during the same period.[18] In addition to this fall at nominally corresponding A-level points, there have been widespread worries that the A-level 'gold standard' has also depreciated. At the same time, arts courses gained esteem because of higher entrance requirements, reflecting the higher calibre of applicants to these courses.

Increases in the proportion of engineering students admitted to universities with low A-level grades have been accompanied by problems in maintaining university standards; the need for new students in engineering to take remedial courses in mathematics is now a frequent complaint of university teachers, and an additional university year is now often

---

[16] Germany is higher than Switzerland in this respect, at least partly because of the greater importance of vehicle production in Germany (see p. 13 above). The figures for science and engineering degrees given in *Education at a Glance: OECD Indicators* (3rd edition, OECD, Paris 1995), tables R12–15 (pp. 218–26) are unfortunately not suitable for our purposes because there are (effectively) no first degrees in Switzerland corresponding to our bachelor degrees.

[17] We use the term 'university' in this case to denote the 'old' (pre-1993) universities only (not polytechnics).

[18] UCCA returns, as summarised by the Engineering Council (mimeo, 1993). The available figures relate to *acceptances* of students' applications by the institutions concerned; since students with higher A-level grades are likely to receive more acceptances than those with lower A-level grades, the numbers with high A-level grades actually taking up their offers and *admitted* to engineering degree courses are likely to be even lower in relation to students with low A-level grades than the above figures suggest.

suggested as necessary if students are to reach hitherto accepted university graduation standards.[19] The issue of quality is important in relation to comparisons of Britain with Switzerland (as with many other Continental countries) since Swiss university-level first qualifications are based on courses that usually are substantially longer than in Britain, and are closer in standard to somewhere between our Master and Doctorate qualifications than to our Bachelor degrees.[20] It is thus not altogether surprising to find that the number of personnel engaged in research and development in Switzerland, at 14.2 per thousand of the workforce, was half as high again as in the United Kingdom (9.2 per thousand) – and higher than in any of the score of countries for which OECD compiled science and technology indicators for 1991; nevertheless some of Swiss industry's demand for highly qualified personnel is met today by employing specialists with high qualifications gained in other countries.[21]

Summary

In this chapter we have seen that the vocational qualifications of the workforce in Switzerland and Britain are radically different. The largest difference between the two countries arises at the lower-intermediate (craft) level, where the proportion of the total *stock* of persons qualified to that

---

[19] R. Sutherland and S. Pozzi, *The Changing Mathematical Background of Undergraduate Engineers* (Engineering Council, 1995).

[20] G. Williams, British higher education in the world league, *Oxford Review of Economic Policy*, 1992, no. 2, gives an account of the many stumbling blocks in the path of international comparisons. He quotes average lengths of 7.4 years for a Swiss degree, and 3.8 for a British degree (France is shown at 5.9, Germany at 9.2 and Italy at 13.6!). The standard length of a Swiss university degree is 5 years, but students on the whole take considerably longer because there is great flexibility in the way students sequence their courses and undertake part-time employment (in their 'technical universities' the standard length is shorter and less flexible at 4 years; at the HTL technical colleges, only 3 years are now required for their basic qualification). For further discussion of numbers in Germany and Britain obtaining university degrees in engineering and selected science subjects, see also G. Mason, *High-level skills and industrial competitiveness: postgraduate engineers and scientists in Britain and Germany*, NIESR Report No. 6, 1994.

[21] *OECD Jobs Study*, part 1, p. 155.

level accounts for the majority of the workforce in Switzerland, and is about six times as high as in Britain. Current *flows* of persons obtaining craft-qualifications in five major occupational groups were 4–5 times as high in Switzerland as in Britain (in proportion to the total age group) at the beginning of this decade. The establishment in Britain in 1986 of a new National Council for Vocational Qualifications has not so far been followed by any increase in numbers qualifying; the available figures indicate an apparent decline.

Some counterbalance has been provided by recent very sharp increases in Britain in university-level education. While *stocks* of university graduates in the workforce are now roughly of equal proportion in Switzerland and in Britain (11 per cent in Britain, 10 per cent in Switzerland), current flows of persons graduating are considerably higher in Britain (19 per cent in Britain, 11 per cent in Switzerland). Worries in Britain with this end of the attainment range are now not as much quantitative as qualitative; in particular, standards of attainment of those admitted to engineering degree courses are falling.

The greatest part of Britain's problem remains at craft level, and it is to this that the ensuing chapters in this book are devoted: we need to examine in practical detail how the Swiss education and training systems operate to yield such a high proportion with vocational qualifications. The next chapter contrasts the schooling systems of the two countries; it considers especially the attainments of, and care given to, lower-attaining pupils and the emphasis on vocationally related elements in the school curriculum. Vocational guidance to school-leavers in the two countries to ensure that they enter suitable apprenticeship occupations is compared in chapter 3. The detailed steps taken to ensure that vocational training is at a high level and of high repute are examined in chapter 4. The final chapter surveys current problems and developments, and suggests priorities that, it is hoped, will be found relevant in discussions of Britain's current policies in these areas.

2 Schooling as preparation for life and work

Pupils' attainments and school organisation

The attainments of the Swiss schooling system attracted international admiration following Switzerland's participation for the first time in 1991 in international tests in mathematics and science set to large representative samples of 13-year-old pupils. These tests – known as the International Assessment of Educational Progress (IAEP) – were taken by pupils in some twenty countries under the sponsorship of the US Department of Education (they were carried out by the Education Testing Service of Princeton, New Jersey, an organisation with much experience of testing in the US). Broadly speaking, Switzerland obtained the highest *average* scores in mathematics; and the scores attained by the *lowest tenth* of all Swiss pupils were very far ahead of the corresponding proportion of pupils in Britain as well as all other countries in that survey.[1] Tests in science showed Swiss pupils at a similar advantage. Swiss methods of schooling, it seems, have led to both higher and more equal attainments than in Britain. Because of the now widely acknowledged need to improve schooling attainments in Britain, particularly for pupils of average or below-average ability, the finding for low-attainers makes Switzerland of very great interest here.

Switzerland has long been blessed with a number of educational thinkers who have acquired international renown: Rousseau, Pestalozzi and

---

[1] Certain exceptions to this broad summary may be footnoted. China recorded higher scores, but only half of all pupils there – presumably the more academic half – are at school at age thirteen. Korea and Taiwan recorded very slightly higher average scores than Switzerland; but for the lowest tenth of pupils Switzerland was still far ahead. Results recorded for such newly developing countries in international tests are impressive; but the cultural gap makes it difficult to draw policy conclusions relevant to Britain.

Froebel were reformers active in the eighteenth and nineteenth centuries (Froebel worked for a decade with Pestalozzi before returning to his native Germany; his writings subsequently had great influence in German-speaking Switzerland). In the twentieth century, Binet and Piaget carried out fundamental work on the measurement and development of children's intelligence and capabilities. Pestalozzi's emphasis two hundred years ago on fostering arithmetical attainments at an early age remains of interest today in the light of the IAEP survey (just mentioned) showing Swiss pupils' outstanding performance in mathematics and, as we shall see later in this chapter, particularly in arithmetic.[2] The ideals and reforms of these early Swiss educationists may be said, in a word, to be directed towards giving teachers a better understanding of a child's intellectual and emotional development, promoting a closer teacher–pupil relationship, and organising teaching so that it takes place – as near as may be possible – in a family atmosphere.[3] Reliance on rote learning in very large classes (50–100 pupils per teacher were often mentioned in descriptions of schooling in the nineteenth century) was to be replaced by more individual 'child-centred' tasks in which children were encouraged to discover things for themselves but, it needs to be emphasised because of recent changes in British teaching practice, essentially *under the detailed guidance of their teacher*. The new methods were of course more expensive; nevertheless, they gradually

[2] K. Silber, *Pestalozzi: The Man and his Work* (Routledge & Kegan Paul, London, 1960); Pestalozzi's methods of teaching arithmetic through contextual examples of carefully graded difficulty were better known in England in the nineteenth century than today as a result of visits on behalf of the educational authorities by J.P. Kay-Shuttleworth to Switzerland and other Continental countries (see his *Four Periods of Public Education*, Longmans, 1862). A school primer in mathematics based on Pestalozzi's principles was issued in English in 1844 under the stimulus of Kay-Shuttleworth with the title *Exercises in Arithmetic for Elementary Schools after the Methods of Pestalozzi*; it was published 'Under the Sanction of the Committee of Council on Education' by J.W. Parker. It formed part of the teacher training programme at Battersea Teachers' Training College in subsequent decades. The level of difficulty in that primer varied from the beginner's '3 from 7 and 4 remain' (p. 7); multi-stage exercises on fractions, 'how many sixths are there in 4 times the $\frac{1}{2}$ of $\frac{1}{3}$ and twice the $\frac{1}{3}$ of $\frac{1}{2}$? [Ans. $\frac{6}{6}$] (p. 120); to volumes, 'the base of a block of stone is 2ft by 3ft, and the length is 5ft; how many cubic feet does it contain?' (p. 171).

[3] On the unifying of family and school life as a prime objective of the approach of Pestalozzi and his followers, see the remarks of R. Lassahn in the proceedings of the 38th *Gemener Kongress* (Deutscher Pedagogik- und Hochschulverlag, Krefeld, 1988), p. 69.

influenced teaching methods in all countries. Remarkably enough, they seem to have been taken further in Britain (especially following the Plowden reforms of 1967) than in Switzerland; it is as if the greater native caution of the Swiss, or their better feeling for a *balance* of teaching approaches, has avoided excesses which have recently caused concern in Britain. In particular, the need for teachers actively to *guide* pupils' learning (emphasised by both Pestalozzi and Froebel) still remains clearly evident in Swiss classrooms, whereas in England that approach has been replaced to a great extent by individualised methods in which the teacher spreads his time – inevitably too thinly – among his many individual charges.[4]

Our visits to Swiss schools in 1992–5 permitted us to observe directly the differences in pupils' attainments recorded in the IAEP tests, and to attempt to identify contributory factors. As mentioned in chapter 1, our visits were carried out jointly with experienced English school inspectors, headteachers and senior teachers from English schools; there have also been reciprocal visits by Swiss teachers and educationists. It goes without saying that not everything that is different abroad is necessarily better, nor necessarily transferable to other countries; but it remains worth recording those differences in schooling organisation and in teaching methods that appear to bear most significantly on pupils' attainments, and to assess which of them might provide pointers for improvements that could be applied here.

The Swiss educational authorities helped in selecting both below-average and above-average schools (in terms of pupils' social background, family problems, immigrant proportions) so that an impression of the average level and of the variability of schooling could be obtained; other schools were selected by using a telephone directory and the 'proverbial pin'. The schools visited were mainly in the city and Canton of Zürich – a world-renowned financial, commercial and industrial centre in the German-speaking part of the country (population of the city, 0.3m.; of the Canton, 1.2m.); other

---

[4] While pupils may benefit by *starting* from self-developed concepts and methods, as a Swiss teacher put it, they need to be led (*geführt*) to optimal methods by the teacher – not simply to carry on working things out by themselves (*nicht man sie einfach rechnen lässt*). The way Froebel's original ideas subsequently influenced teaching in Britain is explained by J. Leibschner, *The Foundations of Progressive Education* (Lutterworth, Cambridge, 1991), p. 154 *et seq*. For a fascinating recent account of the adoption of progressive methods in English primary schools, see R. Alexander, *Innocence and Experience: Reconstructing Primary Education* (ASPE, Trentham NJ, 1994).

schools were visited in Aargau, Bern and St Gallen, also German-speaking. As noted in chapter 1, about three quarters of all Swiss inhabitants have German as their mother tongue; within the limitations of this study, it seemed better not to complicate the picture by including schools from the French and Italian sections of the country.

A total of over fifty complete lessons, and very many more partial lessons, were observed in about twenty Swiss secondary schools by our teams (each team consisting of 2–5 persons). Discussions were also held with teacher training colleges, career guidance specialists, and training officers in large firms; the broad object was to obtain a view of the foundation provided during secondary schooling for subsequent vocational training and employment. Our discussions related both to the details of what was actually observed in each school, and the extent to which they could be regarded as typical; in this way we obtained broader views of current realities.[5] We were also able to discuss changes in schooling that might be desirable in the light of current developments in technology and in international competition.

Britain's greatest shortfall in qualified employees, as we have seen in the previous chapter, is at the craft level. Vocational training at that level for many occupations requires that the school-leaver has solid foundations in subjects such as mathematics, science and practical subjects. It is on these subjects that we focused our visits. We also focused on pupils in the lower half of the academic attainment range; in the past these young people could take up unskilled and semi-skilled jobs, but increasing automation of production has meant that such jobs have gradually diminished in number, and are likely to continue diminishing. The long-standing concern to raise the attainments of below-average school-leavers in Britain has thus become increasingly pressing; it was the teaching and attainments of such pupils that consequently engaged much of our concern on our visits abroad.[6]

---

[5] Schools were visited in both countries in a wide range of settings varying, for example, from industrial urban immigrant areas to rural areas; because of greater concerns in Britain with schooling problems in inner-city areas, our sample was probably overweighted in that direction. Given limited time and resources, our objective was more to obtain a comparative view of schools facing similar problems than to obtain precisely representative samples of the whole of each country's schools.

[6] For further historical background, see SJP's Keynes Lecture to the British Academy in its *Proceedings*, 1993.

Structure of schooling

Before comparing school-leaving standards, it is necessary to outline some basic structural features of the Swiss schooling system. Control of schooling in Switzerland is devolved to grass-root levels to a surprising degree: each of the 26 Cantons prides itself on its own educational legislation, and many Cantons require plebiscites on detailed decisions at the level of the school district. Among such decisions are, for example, the election by popular vote of individual teachers in local school districts to their position for six years at a time, and the introduction of experimental comprehensive schools. While there is much detailed variation among Cantons, many central features of the schooling system observed in Zürich can be regarded for the purpose of the present inquiry as indicative of the German-speaking areas of Switzerland as a whole.

Primary schools in Switzerland cover the full ability range without streaming, as is equally usual in England. Pupils enter primary school in Zürich at the beginning of the school-year after the age of 6¼ (following a school-readiness appraisal, if required); they attend primary school for six years, that is, till age twelve – a year later than usual in England. They then transfer to one of four main types of secondary school: *Oberschulen*, which now cater for about the lowest 5–10 per cent of pupils (apart from pupils in special schools; *Oberschulen* previously catered for the lowest 15 per cent); *Realschulen*, which cater for about the next 35 per cent; *Sekundar-schulen*, which cater for the next 45 per cent; and *Gymnasien* which cater for approximately the top 10–15 per cent. In addition, a variety of special schools and special classes cater for children with learning disabilities and special educational needs.[7] There

7   Special schools and, more importantly, special classes within normal schools cater for a slightly higher proportion of all pupils than in Britain, say 3–4 rather than 1–2 per cent. This difference between the two countries is quantitatively small, at only half a child per class on average; nevertheless, the difference is worth noting as one of the ways in which the task of the teacher in the majority of schools is made more manageable in Switzerland. The movement towards the integration of children with special educational needs into mainstream classes is advancing at a more measured pace in Switzerland than in Britain, with continued provision in Switzerland of trained SEN teachers for tuition of such children *outside* their main classroom (not *inside*, as so often in Britain). The problems associated with integration, and the lack of an adequate research base of knowledge, are surveyed in an OECD report, *The Integration of Disabled Children into Mainstream Education: Ambitions, Theories and Practice* (Paris, 1994); for the Swiss situation, there is a valuable discussion in the volume edited by A. Bürli and G. Bless, *Schulische Integration behinderte Kinder* (Edition SZH, Luzern, 1994).

are further opportunities to transfer to a *Gymnasium* after the second and third years at *Sekundarschule* (about a third of those leaving *Gymnasium* are late-entrants of this type).[8] Compulsory schooling normally ends at age 15; but if a pupil has entered late, or repeated a year, he often stays for an additional year to complete the normal three years of obligatory secondary schooling.

Entry to obligatory schooling is thus some eighteen months later than in England (where attendance usually begins in the *term* before a child reaches his fifth birthday – though many enter at the beginning of the previous school *year*); wealthy as Switzerland is, obligatory full-time schooling normally extends for only nine years ending at age fifteen, whereas in England it extends for eleven years ending at age sixteen.[9] In practice, however, almost all Swiss children attend kindergarten on a part-time basis (2–4 hours a day) for two years before obligatory schooling, that is, at ages 4–6; and many English children begin nursery at age four. The difference between the countries in length of *actual* attendance is thus not quite as great as it may at first seem.

Our visiting teams of English teachers and inspectors frequently commented on the friendlier social relations and evident absence of tension (or 'antagonism') between pupils and teachers in Swiss classrooms; a family-like atmosphere is an integral objective of Pestalozzian schooling and seemed to contribute to better learning. The following general organisational factors seem relevant. Secondary schools in Switzerland are considerably smaller than in England, with 250–500 pupils rather than the thousand or so typical of English comprehensive secondary schools; this immediately contributes to a more intimate atmosphere. Class sizes are smaller, but only slightly: averages of eighteen pupils in Switzerland and twenty-two pupils in England were recorded by the IAEP survey. Some of the current difference in class sizes is due to fluctuations in the birth rate. The fall in the Swiss

---

[8] Pupils who transfer after the third year (class 9) at *Sekundarschule* have to repeat the ninth class at the *Gymnasium*. There is also the possibility for pupils to transfer to the third class of the *Sekundarschule* after completing the third class at the *Realschule*, that is, to repeat the third class of secondary school at a higher-level school; this possibility is rarely taken up.

[9] As said, the account given here relates to Zürich; among the more significant variations in other Cantons, from an English point of view, is age of entry to obligatory schooling. In some Cantons (for example, Grisons) it is a year later than in Zürich, and thus over two years later than in England. Nevertheless, the final outcomes for pupils' attainments in all the areas distinguished in the IAEP analyses are significantly higher than in England (v. fns. 18 and 45 below).

birth rate in the past generation was rather sharper than in Britain (a fall in 1970–85 of 25 per cent in Switzerland, compared with 15 per cent in Britain) and has been followed by a sharper rise in Switzerland since 1985 (12 per cent rise in 1985–90 in Switzerland, compared with 6 per cent in Britain); an increase in class sizes is now expected in Switzerland.

Probably of most importance in determining classroom atmosphere is the greater role of the form teacher in the Swiss pupil's life. The Swiss form teacher in *Realschulen* (a) teaches the majority of subjects, and (b) takes the same group of pupils for three years at a time, that is, throughout compulsory secondary schooling from age twelve to fifteen. In *Sekundarschulen* there are two main teachers, one for arts and another for sciences (including mathematics), and both take the same group of pupils for three years (other details are footnoted).[10] The important consequence is that the Swiss form teacher knows the strengths and weaknesses of his individual pupils far, far better than usually possible for an English form teacher (or for the pastoral tutor who has such responsibilities delegated to him in English secondary schools). The Swiss form teacher is able to notice a pupil's problems at an earlier stage, can deal better with them on an individual basis, and can organise his class – in terms of seating arrangements and the distribution of his attention – so that the class as a whole advances with fewer distractions (we return to these aspects later in this chapter when we discuss teaching styles).

The closer understanding of pupils developed by a Swiss form teacher is particularly important for *Realschule* pupils. A greater proportion of such pupils come from problem families; as teachers frequently told us, such pupils particularly benefit in their social adjustment and cognitive development from the additional support a Swiss form teacher can give them because of the better insight he develops into their individual problems and latent capabilities.[11]

---

[10] In both these school types specialist teachers may take music, gymnastics, and textile work. Only in *Gymnasien* are subject specialists employed, as is normal practice for most subjects in secondary schools in Britain.

[11] Of course there are risks attached to a policy of putting pupils into the hands of a single teacher for a number of years; some teachers are inevitably less experienced than others, some may fail to develop good relations with particular pupils, and some teachers may (rightly) be on the verge of changing their careers. It is possible that our eyes were more successfully distracted from less than wholly happy classes in Switzerland than in England; but, for what it is worth, we have to say that our teams were left in little doubt that the Swiss system only rarely provided even *mild* worries on this account, whereas the current system in Britain raised many

While our main concern in this chapter is with pupils' cognitive attainments, it deserves adding that Swiss teachers place much emphasis on pupils' development as responsible social beings. Through classroom discussion and activities involving 'role play', Swiss teachers often focus on occurrences where they can promote the amicable resolution of conflict situations and the democratic acceptance of classroom rules to improve the learning environment. As part of what is called *Menschenbildung* – perhaps translatable as 'learning to become a civilised human being' – the Zürich curriculum document explicitly lists among the duties of a teacher: encourage pupils' willingness to accept social responsibility in a democratic framework; promote discussion to encourage mutual understanding; encourage recognition of the value of a transmitted common tradition and spiritual heritage, together with an open acceptance of other cultures; promote the use of leisure time for reflection and self-motivation to understand and help others.[12] Taken by themselves these phrases may seem self-evident, and perhaps to overemphasise aspects taken for granted everywhere; our visits left us in little doubt that the promotion of such values at schools was taken further in Swiss than in English schools, and that it was advantageous to do so. Appendix C provides examples of the Swiss view of the teacher as social pedagogue; in view of the problems associated with the continuing increase of single-parent families, these aspects of Swiss schooling, we believe, warrant careful study in Britain.

To some politically sensitive readers, the allocation of pupils to various levels of secondary schooling on the basis of their attainments at primary school carries an old-fashioned and politically disreputable flavour: 'it can be viewed as an elitist practice and contrary to democratic principles', as that side of the argument was expressed in a recent educational reference

---

serious worries as to the proportion of pupils who were being inadequately taught. Without going into the wider implications for the training of teachers of a policy requiring a greater proportion of teachers to be generalists rather than specialists, it is perhaps worth noticing that the broader subject coverage in schools at ages 16–18 required for the Swiss *Matura* (in line with their neighbouring countries) provides a better foundation for the training of generalists than our A-levels (based usually on only two or three subjects). This is not to say that the benefits of early specialisation in depth provided by our A-levels should be given up by all pupils: however, for those planning a career as school teachers, the broader route should be a valued option.

[12] *Lehrplan für die Volkschule des Kantons Zürich* (EDK, Zürich, 1991), pp. 3–5.

book.[13] Nevertheless, it seems agreed on all sides that there is a dilemma in that the variability of pupils' attainments increases with age, while teaching and learning in classes of widely dispersed attainments becomes increasingly difficult. The issue is thus not *whether* schooling should diversify at older ages, but rather: at what ages, and in what ways, should schooling diversify so that young people of different abilities and of different interests are best catered for? From an objective and scientific point of view, given the extraordinary success of the Swiss economy, our need in this study is to understand the degree of success of pupils' attainments under the Swiss schooling system, and to ask which of its structural features can be considered as contributing to its success; none of this vitiates any decision as to the political desirability or undesirability of various types of selective secondary schooling.

In view of the widespread reliance on comprehensive secondary schools in Britain, and moves towards such schools in other countries, it is of interest that in the past 15–20 years a few comprehensive schools (called AVO schools)[14] have been established on an experimental basis in certain school-districts in the Canton of Zürich with the aim of catering more flexibly for pupils' individual strengths and weaknesses, and improving social cohesion. These schools are closer to Britain's earlier (1970s) multilateral schools (in which for most subjects pupils were grouped in the same stream appropriate to their *general* level of attainment) than to its current integrated comprehensive mixed-ability schools in which pupils are separated into 'sets' according to their attainments in only a few subjects (commonly, only mathematics and the first foreign language) and are otherwise taught in mixed ability groups. The Zürich AVO schools cater for all secondary school pupils in the relevant school districts apart from those going to *Gymnasien* and special schools, that is, for about 80–85 per cent of the age group.

---

[13] *The International Encyclopedia of Teaching and Teacher Education* (ed. M.J. Dunkin, Pergamon, Oxford, 1987, p. 225; article by Calfee and Piontkowski). The OECD's series of *Reviews of National Policies for Education* reported for the first time on *Switzerland* in 1991 (English edn), with similar critical remarks – sometimes amusing but hardly scientifically objective. The Swiss secondary schooling system was written off as 'archaic' (p. 26), without consideration of its remarkable achievements. 'It is well known that mountain peoples are concrete and practical and do not like vague concepts or too much talk. Above all, they are inclined to action: not precipitate but thought out, always moving cautiously and with a margin of safety' (p. 55). The chief *Rapporteur* for the OECD *Review* was a French industrial sociologist, Professor J.J. Silvestre, of Aix-en-Provence.

[14] See Appendix D, fn. 2.

Pupils at these AVO schools are divided into two streams, a 'basic level' and an 'extended level', in place of the threefold division into *Oberschule*, *Realschule* and *Sekundarschule*. This division applies to classes for most subjects; but in mathematics and the first foreign language (usually French), pupils are set into three attainment groups, not necessarily the same for the two subjects.[15] Only about a tenth of all secondary pupils in the Canton of Zürich go to these experimental schools.

There is as yet no consensus about the academic success of this experiment. Appendix D summarises the results of comparisons carried out in 1984–7 by the Zürich Education Department of pupils' mathematical attainments under the AVO experimental comprehensive system and the traditional selective systems; these comparisons suggested a slight *lowering* of attainments under the experimental comprehensive system for pupils at both ends of the attainment range – broadly speaking, those in the top half and bottom fifth. Possible reasons are a less central role of the form-teacher in AVO schools; a greater proportion of time spent on outside socialising projects; and less homework. Further comparisons of this type are to be carried out in 1996 (additional analysis, as explained in that Appendix, seems desirable). Of course, even such declines may be a small price for greater social cohesion and other socio-political objectives; these are not matters on which we can or need enter here. Decisions as to whether this system is to be adopted in the remainder of the Canton are due to be taken by popular vote in local communities (*Gemeinde*) in the coming years.

Mathematics

Poor school attainments in mathematics, particularly in arithmetic, have long been recognised as a major obstacle for British school-leavers in taking up vocational training. This is probably the main reason why, in considerable contrast to Switzerland, school-leavers in Britain with average or below-average attainments are virtually barred from craft-level training (NVQ Level 3) in engineering and other technical occupations.

As indicated at the beginning of this chapter, international mathematics tests (the IAEP tests) permitting an estimation of the size of the gap between the two countries were carried out in 1991; some 75 mathematical questions were put to samples of 13-year-olds, which included 3,600 pupils in

---

[15] In AVO schools with many immigrant pupils, the study of German is treated as if it were the foreign language for the purposes of grouping pupils into three sets.

Switzerland, 900 in England and Wales and 1,600 in Scotland.[16] The overall score attained by the median Swiss pupil was attained only by the top-quartile English pupil; this is probably the simplest summary indicator of the difference between the countries in relation to subsequent possibilities of vocational training. In other words, the *average* Swiss pupil reached what used to be called in England 'Grammar school standards' (Grammar schools catered for roughly the top quarter of the ability range). Similarly noteworthy is that the score attained by the Swiss pupil at the lowest quartile was attained only by the median pupil in England; and the score of the lowest-decile pupil in Switzerland was attained by pupils only at about the thirtieth percentile in England. On that last criterion, it may be said – in obviously simplified terms – that there are three times as many low-attaining pupils in England as in Switzerland.[17] Little difference was recorded between the top-decile pupils in the two countries; that may be because the IAEP tests did not adequately discriminate among attainments at that level (the top-decile pupil scored 92 per cent in Switzerland and 88 per cent in England), but it is also consistent with our own classroom observations that the gap widens among lower attainers.

A more detailed analysis of the IAEP results by school type carried out for Zürich confirmed in institutional terms the Swiss advantage in mathematics: *Realschule* pupils, that is, those who were in schools catering roughly for the *lowest third* of the academic attainment range, attained

---

[16] A.E. Lapointe, N.A. Mead and T.M. Askew, *Learning Mathematics* (Educational Testing Service, Princeton NJ, 1992); hereafter IAEP Mathematics. Calculators were not allowed. The tests were carried out in a fixed period of time, usually one school period of 45 minutes (curiously, 'the results of students who omitted questions at the ends of sections because they did not reach them were excluded from the calculations [of 'per cent correct'] for those questions'; *ibid.*, p. 141). For brevity, in relation to IAEP samples we have here used the words 'England', 'English', and so on, to denote England and Wales. The IAEP results for Scotland were sufficiently close to those for England and Wales not to warrant reporting them separately in the following summary account.

[17] These summary and approximate indications of the gap between the countries were derived by graphical interpolation from the percentile scores tabulated in the IAEP report, p. 145, supplemented by unpublished information on medians (61.2 and 77.3, unadjusted for guessing) kindly provided by Dr Mead. The interpolated results quoted in the text above are after adjusting the original published scores for guessing (using the conventional formula) on the basis that 71 per cent of the questions were multiple choice.

average scores above those attained by the average pupil in *all* schools in Britain (a score of 57 compared with 51 per cent).[18]

The representativeness of the English sample was much less satisfactory than the Swiss sample in that only under half (47 per cent) of English pupils selected on a representative basis actually participated, compared with 80 per cent in Switzerland.[19] Schools with poor attainments are less likely to cooperate, partly because teachers in such schools are too busy coping with their heavier burden of problem-pupils, and partly because teachers are not particularly proud of the results of their efforts; it is thus no more than realistic to suspect that the true gap between the two countries' attainments is even larger than appears from the published results of this survey.[20]

The following examples from the IAEP tests illustrate the nature and extent of English pupils' shortfalls in basic arithmetic. The average of seven temperature values (9, 7, 6, 0, 2, 8, and 10°C) was correctly identified by 67 per cent of Swiss pupils compared with only 37 per cent of British pupils. A subtraction problem $1003 - \square = 172$ was correctly solved by 72 per cent of Swiss pupils; the British proportion was 39 per cent. Calculations

---

[18] Urs Moser, *Was wissen 13-jährige? Schulische Leistungen und Schulstrukturen* (Amt für Bildungsforschung der Erziehungsdirektion des Kantons Bern, c. 1992), p. 23. Analyses by main population areas show Zürich pupils as having similar attainments to those in French-speaking areas and in Ticino; but the Canton of Bern performed significantly less well (*ibid.*, p. 16; nevertheless, even Bern was ahead of England).

[19] IAEP Mathematics, p. 135.

[20] That low-attaining schools are less likely to participate emerged from a series of earlier UK studies (see for example, D. Foxman, *Learning Mathematics and Science: The Second International Assessment of Mathematics and Science in England*, National Foundation for Educational Research, Slough, 1992, p. 3 and n. 6). In an attempt to estimate the size of the response bias in the IAEP survey, NFER kindly cooperated with our request to compute adjustment factors based on published GCSE attainments of schools that were *approached* for the IAEP survey and of those schools that eventually *participated*. The originally published score for the lowest decile of 34.5 (unadjusted for guessing, IAEP Mathematics, p. 145) was consequently lowered to 32. This method of allowing for bias in England can be regarded as only partial for the following reason. While most countries took a representative sample of pupils throughout the attainment range in each school, the procedure in England was based on sampling whole classes; classes in mathematics in English comprehensive schools are usually 'set' on the basis of ability, and it consequently seems likely that there were additional biases *within* schools as a result of lower response by low-attaining *classes*. The method of adjustment adopted here accounts, at a guess, for perhaps no more than half the total bias.

involving decimals present great difficulties to English pupils, and provided the most striking contrasts: 69 per cent of Swiss pupils were able to identify the correct decimal number equal to 5/8, compared with 21 per cent of British pupils; 56 per cent of Swiss pupils, but only 14 per cent of British pupils, were able to name the smallest of four specified decimal numbers below unity (0.625, 0.25, 0.3753, 0.125); multiplying 9.2 by 2.5 was carried out correctly by 55 per cent of Swiss pupils, but by a mere 13 per cent of British pupils.[21]

It is sometimes said that performance in arithmetic by pupils in Britain may be lower than in other countries, but that British pupils 'compensate' for that weakness by better performance in other branches of mathematics, for example, geometry or data handling. The IAEP survey indicates that it is more accurate to say, not that British pupils are better, but that their shortfall is not as great in other branches of mathematics as in arithmetic. Of all questions classified under arithmetic ('number and operations') in the IAEP tests, the percentage of correct answers by Swiss pupils was 67, compared with 49 by English pupils. The gap in questions classified under 'measurement' (for example, the circumference of rectangles, or the volume of cubes) was slightly smaller: 53 per cent of Swiss pupils, and 40 per cent of British pupils, answered such questions correctly. In questions relating to 'algebra' 54 per cent of Swiss pupils answered correctly, compared with 43 per cent of British pupils. In 'geometry' the percentages correct were 71 per cent for Switzerland, and 63 per cent for Britain.

'Data analysis, probability and statistics' was the only branch in which the difference in attainment between the two countries could be described as negligible: 78 per cent of Swiss pupils answered correctly, compared with 75 per cent of British pupils. In contrast to Britain, very little explicit emphasis is placed on this branch of mathematics in Swiss schools. Probability and statistics are not taught at that age in Switzerland (note, however, the example on averages mentioned above), nor is much weight given to 'tables and graphs'.[22] Nevertheless, the advantage – slight as it may be – lay with the Swiss; it might therefore properly be asked whether the time invested in explicitly teaching these topics to British pupils at young ages would be better used by giving greater emphasis to basic arithmetic.

[21] All except the last of these questions were multiple choice with four possible answers; the 'percentages correct' quoted in this and the immediately following paragraphs have been adjusted for guessing (see fn. 17; a more accurate calculation would take into account that the proportions varied according to topic).

[22] Similarly in Japan, probability and statistics are not part of the school curriculum at this age but are deferred till 17–18.

Our teams' observations of Swiss *Realschule* classrooms confirmed the picture recorded by the IAEP survey: English teachers and school inspectors were consistently surprised that nominally 'low-attaining' pupils in Switzerland were working at standards comparable to those expected of pupils in middle-level sets in good English schools. That judgement referred as much to the mastery of curriculum content as to the consistency, orderliness and clean presentation in pupils' exercise books. A greater concentration on arithmetic seems to characterise Swiss teaching; there is also greater emphasis on three-dimensional conceptualisation linked to technical drawing.

The following examples illustrate the standard of work by pupils that we observed in the final two years of Swiss secondary *Realschulen*, corresponding to Years 9 and 10 in English comprehensive schools in below-average sets. Calculation of the circumference and area of circles was taught to Swiss *Realschule* pupils at age fourteen (corresponding to our Year 9), as also was the construction of a trapezium from given dimensions of certain sides and angles. Under the 1994 revision of the National Curriculum, areas of circles are expected to be taught only to *average*-ability pupils in England a year later at age 15 (Level 6 of the National Curriculum); below-average pupils are expected to be two years further behind (at Level 5).[23] At a *Realschule* which we visited, 15-year-old Swiss pupils (our Year 10) solved problems involving proportions of the kind that arise in 'mixtures'; for example: 'Chocolate type A costs 12 SwFr/kg, chocolate type B costs 21 SwFr/kg. A company wants to produce Easter bunnies, each weighing 250g and selling at SwFr8.20. The cost of the material is to be 50 per cent. Calculate how much of the two types of chocolate will be used.'[24] In Britain problems of this type are expected to be set only to above-average 16-year-olds (NC Level 7 and above). Similarly, the application of Pythagoras is expected to be taught to *Realschule* pupils at age 14–15 in Switzerland, but only to above-average pupils at age sixteen in England (Level 7 of the National Curriculum). These examples, in summary, support the broad judgement reached by our team of inspectors and teachers that in basic mathematical processes Swiss *below-average* pupils were

[23] Under the Dearing proposals of May 1994, areas of circles were recommended to be moved to Level 7, that is, they were thought only suitable for *above-average* 16-year-olds; but in the Order issued at the end of 1994 this topic remained at Level 6 (to which it was moved in 1991; previously in the original 1989 Order, it could be found at Level 8 of AT8).

[24] This type of exercise is on the official curriculum for the final year of *Realschulen*. In practice, only better pupils reach this standard; but the contrast with British pupils even in 'middle sets' is remarkable.

working at a standard that is ahead by a year or two of what is expected in England even of *average* pupils, and considerably further ahead for corresponding English low attainers.

Teaching style

We next describe aspects of teaching methods observed in Swiss mathematics classes which are typically different from our observations of English classes, and which seem to contribute in an important way to pupils' better attainments. Much of what has to be said on these matters applies also to other subjects; but it is well to illustrate the issues in terms of mathematics teaching in which there are particularly serious difficulties in England. That subject – as teachers often say – is more 'linear': what is learnt by a pupil today depends more strongly on what he has learnt yesterday (the learning of foreign languages is similar in this respect). The differences between the countries in this subject are perhaps for that reason particularly clear. We shall deal here with observed differences in teaching styles, and leave to the end of the chapter a consideration of differences in circumstances – mostly beyond the control of the teacher – that may encourage Swiss, but not English, teachers to adopt such methods.[25]

On entering a classroom in Britain, particularly a primary school classroom, pupils are often found dispersed around tables in groups of four to six; some have their backs to the blackboard. They work 'at their own pace' – a fundamental ideal of progressive educationists – through exercises from books, booklets, worksheets or cards; most pupils work individually – even though notionally they are supposed to be 'working in groups'. Pupils within a single classroom are usually at significantly different stages, according to their supposed individual levels of ability, and they may work on different topics and from different books. This applies even in schools where pupils have been 'set' according to their levels of attainment in parallel classes. Whole-class teaching is to be observed for only a small fraction of the lesson time in British mathematics classrooms, particularly rarely in classes for average and below-average pupils. It often takes place for no longer than a few minutes at the beginning of a lesson when the teacher makes organisational announcements, or when a new topic is introduced. For most of the time pupils are left to their own resources. The teacher's role is mainly to help individual pupils when there are difficulties, and to

---

[25] To anticipate in a footnote: the 'underlying circumstances' are the greater evenness of pupils' attainments, and the emphasis placed on the maintenance of that evenness throughout schooling (p. 60 below)

check their work. Pupils are addressed by the teacher usually only if they request it. Often several pupils need the teacher's help at the same time; they therefore put their hands up – or queue at his desk – waiting until the teacher is free to help them. Some teachers have a rule for length of queues, such as 'not more than four waiting at my desk at a time'; other teachers walk around the class with a 'crocodile' of pupils trailing behind them waiting for their questions to be answered. The pressure on teachers means that checking of pupils' work is often cursory; many pupils do not receive adequate support from the teacher to carry out their work successfully, and poor understanding by *pupils* frequently goes unnoticed. Average pupils, and even more so those who are below average, consequently suffer. As HMI recently observed in relation to mathematics classes, the use of individualised teaching programmes 'places undue responsibility on *pupils* for controlling the pace and quality of their learning'; the proportions of pupils who 'were successful in their work' ('on task', as educationists put it), is as low as 50–60 per cent, and this 'did not help motivation'.[26] As many others have said, working 'at their own pace' means for many pupils 'doing as little as you can get away with'; pupils may often behave ostensibly as if they were engaged on their work, but their learning time is not used efficiently.

There is of course considerable variation among schools. At one extreme, virtually no whole-class teaching takes place; and pupils spend much of their lesson time on 'holding activities' which can hardly be recognised as contributing systematically to their progress, for example, joining dots on a grid to make patterns, cutting out triangles and calculating ratios of their sides (a time-absorbing task observed in classes for 16-year-olds).[27] In high-ability sets, whole-class teaching is to be observed more frequently and greater attempts are made to ensure that all pupils in the class work at the same level.[28]

[26] Ofsted, *Science and Mathematics in Schools: A Review* (HMSO, London, 1994), p. 16; and *Mathematics: Key stages 1,2,3 and 4* (HMSO, 1993), paras 19–20 (our emphasis).

[27] The term 'holding activities' (i.e. activities to keep some pupils busy while the teacher deals with others) is used in the Ofsted report (*op. cit.*, 1994), p. 21.

[28] Alternative teaching styles in English mathematics classrooms were described in the Cockcroft report, *Mathematics Counts* (HMSO, 1982), esp. pp. 91–4 and 150–2. The report commends more 'exposition' and 'discussion'; the difficulties of teaching a class divided into groups were recognised, but the discussion is not incisive. The general and fundamental contrast between British and Continental classroom practice was not explained, probably for lack of experience by those who compiled the report (there is one reference to teaching practices in a Danish classroom, but not to other countries, see pp. 103 and 236). See also the critical discussion of 'Cockcroft styles' by J. Backhouse, L. Haggarty, S. Pirie and J. Stratton, *Improving the Learning of Mathematics* (Cassell, London, 1992), p. 129.

The Swiss secondary school classroom is typically different. Desks are often arranged in a 'horseshoe' or similar pattern, with the teacher's desk in the centre of the open end or to the window-side of it, and sometimes with one or two pupils' desks in the middle of the open end to permit pupils with habitual difficulties to be nearer the teacher. There is usually an overhead projector in addition to a blackboard; the main advantage of the OHP, from the teacher's point of view, is that it allows more continuous supervision and eye contact with pupils, since the teacher faces the class while writing. A large part of each lesson – between half and two thirds – is devoted to continuous interaction between the teacher and the whole class. This form of instruction is not a lecture, interspersed with occasional questions by the teacher to pupils – as 'whole-class teaching' is often understood in England; rather, the teacher starts with a realistic problem, and develops solutions and concepts through a series of graded questions addressed to the whole class. Questions may be put every minute or two; the teacher may wait half a minute before calling on a pupil – whether he has raised his hand or not – to answer or write the next step on the blackboard or overhead projector. Pupils are thus guided towards discovering solutions themselves (*fragend entwickeln*).

Virtually the whole class is mentally engaged in the learning process during this oral part of the lesson. From the breadth of response in the class, the teacher is able to judge how far he needs to go in the exposition of difficult steps; and he sees which pupils are likely to require individual help during the subsequent period devoted to written exercises. Only after the oral stage has been adequately mastered is the class asked to carry out written exercises on their own (sometimes continued as homework). Virtually all pupils in the classes we observed completed their work successfully. Grouping of pupils within a class, to permit some form of joint working, was sometimes observed for part of the lesson in Swiss classes: the important contrast with England is that it occupied only a limited fraction of the lesson time.

To English teachers familiar in their mathematics classes with long tails of under-achieving pupils who have trouble in understanding what they are expected to do, the degree of evenness among Swiss *Realschule* pupils in their attainments comes as a considerable revelation as to what lies within the realm of possibility.[29] In Swiss classes catering for the next higher range of abilities – in *Sekundarschulen* – the same style of teaching is employed,

---

[29] The slightly higher proportion of Swiss pupils with separate SEN provision has been noted above (fn. 7); it warrants detailed further investigation as to how much this may contribute to the greater feasibility of whole-class teaching in Swiss schools.

though the approach is more abstract and conceptual. The pace of teaching is faster, partly because of pupils' higher ability; their range of attainments is yet more uniform than in the lower-ability *Realschulen*. In English mathematics classes which have been 'set' by attainment, it might be thought that the middle sets would show a comparably narrow range; but it seems that Swiss teaching methods lead to a distinctly greater uniformity even among such middle-ability groups.

Let us next look at other differences in teaching: textbooks, calculators, investigatory methods, class size and teaching time.

Textbooks

Textbooks are fundamental to the teaching process in most Swiss mathematics classes, even if they are not always visible during the intensive oral phase of the teaching process that occupies most of the lesson time, and even if considerable supplementary material is sometimes introduced by a particular teacher.[30] The textbooks are significantly different in construction, and used differently, from those familiar in England. English pupils' textbooks are more in the nature of self-instruction ('teach yourself') manuals. Swiss pupils' textbooks – usually a single book for each year of schooling – contain little self-instruction material but plenty of exercises; and they are thinner (comparing the textbooks required by a pupil for the whole year). There is a textbook for each level of schooling (similar to the yellow, red, blue and green versions of some English textbook series for pupils of different levels).[31] Most important, a thick teacher's manual accompanies each textbook; it provides detailed suggestions for teaching each page (sometimes, pair of pages) in the pupils' book, including the precise teaching aims, master copies for OHP transparencies, and often a suggested year plan indicating which pages are to be covered in each week of the year. Teachers' manuals are also available for many English textbook series, but their nature and use is different – probably because the authors realise that

---

[30] Teaching material is more varied in the Swiss *Gymnasien*.

[31] The English parallel series for different levels of attainment are written in styles descending markedly from the hieratic to the demotic; see P. Dowling, A touch of class: ability, social class and intertext in SMP 11–16 (in D. Pimm and E. Love, eds, *Teaching and Learning School Mathematics*, Hodder and Stoughton, London, 1991, p. 137). The Swiss parallel series, with less intention to act as teach-yourself manuals, display a more even dourness.

there is less whole-class teaching; teachers' manuals in England may be a 'good source of ideas', as HMI recently put it, but 'few teachers referred to these manuals'.[32]

Swiss textbooks are drafted by groups of experienced teachers to cover the prescribed curriculum of the Canton; they are trialled, revised in the light of experience, and then approved by the Cantonal education authorities. The prescribed curriculum is only a brief schematic document which specifies the topics to be covered by the different schooling levels in each year.[33] The authorised textbooks are in the nature of an approved amplification of the legally binding curriculum; they have much the same role as the *Scheme of Work* in English schools – except that in England each school is expected to develop its own *Scheme* in a laborious and difficult attempt to meet the requirements of the National Curriculum. Swiss teachers may choose alternative or supplementary permitted teaching material, and they may place less emphasis on some topics than on others. Variations in attainment between parallel classes in the same school, and among schools of the same level, are noticeably smaller in Switzerland than in England; the predominant use of the same textbook is undoubtedly an important factor.

In English schools, teachers frequently reject the idea of teaching according to a single textbook. They often say that they have not found a single textbook that is adequate in coverage of topics, or in providing sufficient exercises for consolidation. But doctrinal opposition to anything smacking of rote learning is probably at the root. It is as if the use of a main textbook might be taken as evidence that they are failing in their duty of providing a mix of instructional material professionally tailored to the actual mix of pupils' attainments in their class. Some schools use their very own scheme of instruction, transmitted on duplicated sheets from one generation of teachers to the next (much 'reinventing of the wheel' from first principles is to be observed). More frequently, a variety of printed textbooks and workbooks is available in the classroom; but often there are insufficient copies of a single text to be used simultaneously by the whole class (lack of resources is another reason often advanced for not teaching from books). Pupils within a class are therefore commonly to be observed sharing textbooks.

---

[32] Ofsted, *The Teaching and Learning of Numbers in Primary Schools* (HMSO, London, 1993), para. 46.

[33] The latest version of the Zürich curriculum also indicates the depth at which topics are to be taught: (1) introductory, (2) working procedures, (3) mastery (*aufgreifen, durcharbeiten, festigen; Lehrplan für die Volksschule des Kantons Zürich*, 1991, p. 259).

English pupils do not usually take textbooks home: they are available only for use in the class, and are not intended for routine revision outside school hours. Swiss pupils, in contrast, each have their own textbook, and are expected to take them home for their homework. They and their parents know what material is to be covered, and pupils use their books for revision and preparation as necessary.

The foregoing remarks on differences between the two countries in their use of textbooks, while concerned principally with secondary schooling, apply also to the primary phase when the foundations are laid on which much later successful mathematical learning depends. Further work comparing primary mathematics textbooks used in Britain, Switzerland and Germany is in progress at the Institute.[34] The greater attention on the Continent to consolidation of foundations and to mental calculating facility are the overriding themes that have so far emerged from those comparisons.

Calculators

English schooling prides itself on its eagerness to introduce new technology into its classrooms; the requirement to use calculators even in *primary* schools is now embodied in the legally binding provisions of the National Curriculum for England. In secondary schools, as the IAEP survey reported, by the age of thirteen some 90 per cent of English pupils both owned and used a calculator at school; in Switzerland, a similar proportion at that age owned calculators, but only 50 per cent of Swiss pupils of that age *ever* used calculators in school.[35] At younger ages, the long-established view that the mind of the pupil needs thorough training in mental arithmetic has so far remained paramount in Switzerland (as in many other countries, including Japan), and has not been displaced by the advent of the pocket calculator. The problem with electronic calculators is that they *conceal* the process of calculation from the user, and are thus quite different in their educational value from an abacus.

Calculators were in use in almost all mathematics lessons that we observed in English secondary schools. It was not unusual to find several pupils making fairly obvious calculator errors, which went unnoticed by them because of poor capabilities in making advance mental estimates of results. In Switzerland calculators were observed only very exceptionally in primary schools; even in secondary schools they were not visible in most of the class-

---

[34] For preliminary results, see NI Discussion Paper no. 90 by Helvia Bierhoff on Laying the Foundations of Mathematics (1996).

[35] IAEP Mathematics, p. 57.

rooms visited. When they were used in Swiss secondary classes we did not observe the kind of calculator errors observed in English schools at that age; by then Swiss pupils are sufficiently adept in mental arithmetic to assess whether a result obtained by using a calculator is likely to be correct.

Calculators in Swiss classes are used in *Realschulen* and *Sekundarschulen* mainly to enable pupils to obtain a precise result *more quickly* than they could with pencil and paper (for example, division by a multi-digit divisor – a calculation beyond most English secondary school pupils, even to a first approximation, without a calculator). For top-ability pupils in a *Gymnasium* class we observed 15-year-olds using programmable calculators (rather than computers) while being introduced to branching processes and loops in a problem in the theory of games; work at this level was not seen in English schools by pupils at that age.

Computers were not observed as part of systematic mathematics instruction in either country. In England there was frequently a computer in a corner of the room, used by one or two pupils while the rest of the class worked on their various exercises; the most active use of computers observed in English schools was in other subjects, where they were used as word processors. In Swiss *Realschulen*, computers were used in technical drawing classes for 15-year-olds (CAD MacDraw programs).

Investigations

A time-consuming constituent of English school mathematics – conspicuously absent in Switzerland – is laid down in the National Curriculum as Attainment Target 1: it is entitled 'Using and Applying Mathematics' and purports to require pupils to apply their 'mathematical knowledge to practical and real-life situations'. In reality it consists of extended tasks, often open-ended for which there is no single correct answer; its importance is supposed to lie in the *process* rather than the *product* (as educationists put it). A simple example recommended for a mixed-ability class is:-

> Start with any two numbers less than 10 (say 1 and 5). Make a series like this: 1, 5, 6, 1, 7, 8, 5, ... How is this series obtained? What are the next six numbers? Choose other starting numbers, and investigate how many series you can make. What happens if you use numbers in other bases?[36]

[36] From Schools Council, *Mixed-ability Teaching in Mathematics* (Evans/Methuen, London, 1977), p. 36.

High-ability 13-year-olds were given the following task:-

The number 33 can be expressed as the sum of two primes: 33 = 31 +
2. However, 35 cannot be expressed as the sum of *two* primes, although
it can be expressed as the sum of three primes: 35 = 5 + 13 + 17. Investigate the number of primes needed for different numbers.[37]

A 'mathematical' investigation set to 14-year-olds had only a nominal
mathematical content:-

Design and carry out a survey which has something to do with Easter
Eggs.

And 16-year-olds were asked:-

Find the relationship between the *number* of dots inside geometric
shapes drawn by connecting dots arranged in grid form, and the *area*
of those shapes.

The main work to be carried out by pupils in such investigations consists of wordy written accounts of what they plan to do, what they did,
difficulties they encountered (to obtain a good mark, pupils know that it
is important to describe many false starts and false trails), limitations of
their work, and so on.

Exercises of this sort in an English class may serve as convenient 'holding activities', keeping pupils busy while teachers – using their individualistic
teaching methods – try to meet the needs of an over-wide diversity of
pupils' attainments. No such exercises were observed in Swiss classrooms.
This is not to say that Swiss pupils do not carry out exercises which 'use
and apply mathematics' (to use the terminology of the English National
Curriculum); on the contrary – the Swiss approach is to ensure that problems are realistic, but also that they are soluble so that a sufficient number
of problems can be tackled within the available time to ensure mastery (and
even 'over-learning') by virtually all pupils in the class.[38] For example (a

---

[37] This is Vinogradoff's problem of 1937, as yet only partially solved.

[38] The same approach is adopted in the Netherlands where 'realistic' mathematics
(that is, starting from contextual problems) has become an important pedagogi-
cal movement (K. Gravemeijer, M. van der Heuvel and L. Streefland, *Contexts,Free
Productions, Tests and Geometry in Realistic Mathematics Education*, State
University of Utrecht, 1990).

problem for middle-attaining 13-year-olds):

> In 1989 the town of Zürich disposed of 144,695 tonnes of household refuse. How much was produced by each of the 361,000 inhabitants? How many refuse sacks taking 2.5kg on average were filled by a family of four in a year? Suppose the refuse was loaded on a train, in which each wagon takes about 20 tonnes and is 10m long. How long would a train be that could take the refuse of Zürich for the year 1989?[39]

There is of course much to be said in favour of extended projects, in that they enable pupils to exercise their creativity and independence; it applies as much to other subjects (science or technology) as to mathematics. The difficulty in the context of current English teaching practice is that such projects have been inadequately limited in time, at the cost of more systematic learning practices.

Class sizes and teaching time

The main cost of schooling is the number of teachers in relation to the number of pupils. As mentioned, mathematics classes in Switzerland at age thirteen were recorded in the IAEP survey as averaging 18 pupils compared with 22 in England. Our visits to Swiss secondary schools showed some variation in class sizes (up to 25 pupils are permitted per class in Zürich) without any obvious relation to pupils' attainments; the greater evenness of Swiss pupils' attainments seemed the more important factor in making teaching easier for the teacher, and in making learning easier for pupils. Total instruction time for all subjects was much the same in the two countries, but time devoted to mathematics lessons was about a quarter higher in Switzerland than England (250 compared with 190 minutes a week; that is, 16 per cent compared with 12.5 per cent of instruction time); lessons in mathematics were given every day of the school week in England to only

---

[39] From *AVO Math 7 m* (Zürich, prov. ed., 1992), p. 38. The proposed 1994 revision of the English mathematical curriculum, as published for consultation, included a suggestion for integrating the application of mathematics with each of its substantive topics (arithmetic, algebra, geometry). This was opposed by the Royal Society together with academics of the Joint Mathematical Council in a curious way: they 'welcomed the principles of integration' but, in the spirit of Augustine, thought 'the time is not yet appropriate' (RS press release, 9 May 1994). The suggestion was not adopted.

17 per cent of pupils, while in Switzerland 60 per cent of pupils had a mathematics lesson every day.[40] Higher attainments in mathematics in England may thus require, not greater resources in total, but a shift in the balance of the curriculum towards mathematics, together with greater emphasis on teaching that subject each day to provide consistent reinforcement.[41]

Science

In English schools great emphasis is placed on science teaching, not least because of the worryingly low proportion of young people qualifying in engineering and technological occupations (as noted in chapter 1). In an attempt to raise science attainments in England, science has been made an obligatory subject under the National Curriculum for all pupils *starting as early as the age of five*. However, insufficient mathematical skills often make it difficult to teach science – particularly physics – in any valuable depth to English average and below-average pupils even at secondary-school ages. In this section we explain the major differences in science teaching in the two countries on the basis of our classroom observations, taking into account the IAEP test results in that subject.

Time spent and pupils' attainments

The Swiss devote a quarter *less* time in secondary schools to science subjects at age thirteen than in England, amounting to 10 per cent of instruction time compared with 13 per cent in England (152 compared with 194

---

[40] IAEP Mathematics, p. 49. The use of 'double periods' in some schools in England (e.g. twice 35 minutes to form a continuous lesson of 70 minutes in mathematics) lowers the efficiency of learning, since pupils' concentration falls towards the end of such an extended period in mathematics (whereas in practical work a longer period is an advantage). Some secondary schools in England teach mathematics on only two days a week (a 'double period' each time).

[41] Two within-country correlations calculated by IAEP deserve mention: correlations within most countries between pupils' attainments and *frequency of teacher-presentation* were positive; on the other hand, correlations between attainment and *frequency of group-work* were negative (p. 53). That is to say, pupils did better in those classes in which teachers spent more time in active teaching, and they did better in those classes in which less time was devoted to learning in groups. Unfortunately, IAEP did not carry out multiple regression analyses involving other factors simultaneously, nor publish the sizes of regression coefficients.

minutes a week). Taking mathematics and science together, much the same *total* time is devoted to these subjects in both countries (380–400 minutes, or a quarter of total instruction time), but within that total there is a notably greater emphasis in Switzerland on mathematics than on science.[42] Time devoted to science in England in the final two years of schooling usually increases, depending on the choice of optional subjects; most pupils (some 85 per cent) took 'double award' science in 1993–94 which requires some 20 per cent of school time.[43] The time devoted by Swiss pupils in *Real-* and *Sekundarschulen* to science throughout the three years of their secondary schooling is closer to 'single award' science in England which is expected to absorb 10–12 per cent of school time.

Despite the substantially lower time devoted by Swiss pupils to science, the IAEP tests in that subject – carried out in parallel to the mathematics tests mentioned above – showed Swiss pupils attaining substantially higher scores than English pupils. The 64 questions administered to pupils by IAEP covered the broad range of science topics: life sciences, physical sciences, earth and space sciences, nature of science (experimental methods). The score attained by the median Swiss pupil was attained by English pupils only at the top thirtieth percentile of the attainment range (whereas in mathematics it was the top twenty-fifth percentile); and the Swiss pupil at the lowest decile attained a score that in England was attained only above the lowest thirtieth percentile. On that last criterion, it may be said – very much as in mathematics – that there were three times as many very low attaining pupils in sciences in England as in Switzerland.[44] An analysis of the IAEP survey by school types for Zürich confirmed that *Realschule* pupils (as explained, roughly the lowest third by academic attainment) did as well as average pupils in England and Wales.[45]

---

[42] A.E. Lapointe, J.M. Askew and N.A. Mead, *Learning Science* (Educational Testing Service, Princeton NJ, 1992), p. 49 (*IAEP Science* hereafter).

[43] DfE, *Statistical Bulletin 5/94*, para. 12; Ofsted, *Science: Key Stages 1, 2, 3 and 4: Fourth Year, 1992–93* (HMSO, London, 1993), p. 17.

[44] Interpolated graphically from the percentile scores in *IAEP Science*, p. 143, and unpublished information on medians (78.1 and 70.3, unadjusted for guessing). The gap between the countries in science is very slightly narrower than that for mathematics. The poor participation rate by English schools (only 48 per cent of sampled pupils, *ibid.*, p. 133) makes it likely that the true gap between English and Swiss pupils is greater than shown in the IAEP survey (see fn. 17 above).

[45] Moser, *op. cit.*, p. 24. There were no significant differences in science between average attainments in the various Swiss language-areas distinguished in the IAEP analysis (*ibid.*, p. 17).

Demonstrations and own experiments

In considering how to improve pupils' attainments in science, 'it may not be the number of minutes of science instruction that is important, but how that time is used', as the IAEP report on science put it.[46] A stark contrast between England and Switzerland was recorded by the IAEP in the extent to which experiments are conducted by pupils and the extent to which they are demonstrated by the teacher: 83 per cent of English pupils carried out experiments on their own at least once a week, compared with only 24 per cent of Swiss pupils. England had a higher proportion of pupils performing their own experiments than any other country participating in that survey.[47] Within each country, the correlations between pupils' scores in science and the amount of pupil-conducted experiments were on the whole significantly negative; that is to say, within each country, pupils obtained higher scores in those schools which required *less* experimentation by pupils on their own.[48]

The great priority attached in English science classes to *pupils' carrying out their own experiments*, rather than seeing them *demonstrated* by the teacher as part of the teaching process, is in accord with English educationists' interpretation of the doctrine that pupils need to 'discover' the truth for themselves. That priority was embodied, and much extended, in the English National Curriculum for science under Attainment Target no. 1, 'Scientific Investigation' (called 'Experimental and Investigation Science' under the revision of 1994, with associated minor changes in substantive emphasis). This approach has been subject to even sharper criticism than the corresponding investigatory Target in mathematics: in science, pupils are required to develop their *own individual* investigations; such investigations are very time-absorbing, and time is too often used in an unsystematic way from the point of view of inculcating established key scientific facts, relations and theories.[49]

[46] *IAEP Science*, p. 49.

[47] *Ibid.*, pp. 51 and 147.

[48] *IAEP Science*, pp. 50–1. The correlations calculated within each of the participating countries were significantly negative in eleven countries, significantly positive in only one country, and not significantly different from zero in eight countries (including England!). It is a pity that detailed results were not reported for the 'not significant' relations, since they might have been combined to yield a joint result which reached statistical significance.

[49] As HMI recently observed, 'in a significant proportion of lessons ... insufficient attention [is] given to explaining, reinforcing and consolidating key concepts'; see Ofsted, *Science Key Stages 1, 2, 3 and 4* (HMSO, London, 1993), para. 18.

On our visits to English science classes, even when more or less the same science experiments were carried out by a whole class or group of pupils, we observed that time was often not well used. Examples included groups of pupils laboriously 'building an electric motor' from primitive materials – a cotton reel wound with a piece of wire, paper-clips used as pivots and a plastic beaker used as a stand (much time was spent by pupils in trying to balance the 'coil' on the beaker so that it would turn under current). Lengthy measuring experiments, with an emphasis on alternative (but essentially trivial) methods for 'presentation of data', are also typical of English science classes. For example, in a biology lesson concerned with the relative influence of inheritance and environment on human characteristics, most of the lesson time (a 'double lesson' of 70 minutes) was devoted to pupils collecting data on each others' hand sizes, thumb lengths, colour of hair and eyes, and whether or not they could roll their tongue (an inherited characteristic of no known significance – as, indeed, the teacher explained). Pupils were asked to 'think about how to record, analyse and present this information', and additional time was to be spent in the following lesson on pie charts, bar charts, and so on. Currently accepted doctrine in English schooling is that pupils benefit from a 'sense of ownership' of their *own* data; but, as educationists from the University of Leeds noted following extensive observation of English science lessons, 'the alleged benefits of ownership of [pupils'] work are occasionally present, more often not'.[50]

On our visits to English science lessons it was evident that many pupils had gained only a superficial idea of the principles underlying their individual experiments, and some had undoubtedly developed a faulty understanding. Teachers tended to refrain from instructing pupils in the scientific principles at issue; rather, in accordance with views long commended by HMI, they wished to encourage pupils to 'think scientifically for themselves', 'speculate about scientific ideas' and 'pursue their own lines of enquiry'.[51] There may be something to be said in favour of this approach, but it seems to have been taken too far in English schools. In the critical words of the Leeds University educationists: 'very frequently pupils ended an investigation confused or mistaken about the science on which they have

[50] See J.F. Donnelly, A.S. Buchan, E.W. Jenkins and A.G. Welford, *Investigations in Science Education Policy: Sc1 in the National Curriculum for England and Wales* (Centre for Policy Studies in Education, University of Leeds, 1993), esp. pp. 3, 6, 8. Note their remarkably incisive comments on the difficulties created for teachers in having to supervise a diversity of individually-planned activities.

[51] Ofsted, *op. cit.*, paras. 15, 24.

been working'; the present state of English science teaching, they thought, 'undermines ... the fostering of scientific knowledge'.[52]

Pupils' own experiments in Switzerland are more closely guided by the teacher; as remarked to us by Swiss teachers, this is especially important for below-average pupils since they are more easily discouraged if their experiments fail or run into difficulties. Experiments carried out by Swiss pupils are often preceded by a demonstration to the whole class performed by the teacher; subsequently, the teacher involves pupils in the learning process by discussing the implications with the class as a whole on the blackboard or OHP. In other science lessons the Swiss teacher may integrate demonstration with interactive discussion and questioning: pupils are asked to anticipate possible results, explain their reasons for anticipated and actual results, and consider the next experimental step necessary in order to verify those reasons. In these ways Swiss pupils participate more efficiently in the process of 'discovering' scientific relationships. Dictating notes to pupils in a lecturing style, as sometimes observed even in low-attaining science sets in England, was not observed in Switzerland.[53]

Balance of science topics

Styles of teaching, expressed most clearly in terms of the greater role of demonstrated experiments in Switzerland and the smaller role of pupils' own experiments, formed the main difference observed between the two

---

[52] Donnelly *et al.* (*loc. cit.*) also gave the following incisive example: 'We have seen pupils convinced that the "froth" visible in a boiling yeast suspension meant that the enzymes present functioned more effectively at 100°C than at room temperature [when, in truth, the enzymes have been destroyed at that high temperature]. Meanwhile a harassed teacher was either unaware of the situation, or uncertain about the ... legitimacy (sic) in [the currently approved] teaching context, of correcting this impression.'

[53] This variant of whole-class teaching – involving much dictation of notes – may be peculiar to England; it was the only country in the IAEP survey (pp. 50–1) for which a *negative* correlation was reported between pupils' scores and the 'amount of listening to science lessons'. Significant positive correlations were reported for eight other countries. The different character and role of science textbooks and teacher's guides in the two countries deserves fuller treatment than possible in the present context. Such a comparison could profitably begin with the Swiss chemistry textbook and accompanying teacher's guide by H.J. Streiff and K. Bolleter, *Chemie* (LKZ, 1992, pp. 262, 200); these were recognised by English teachers who examined them as providing significantly better aids for teachers and pupils than material currently available here, and worthy of translation into English.

countries' science lessons; that difference, in turn, affected the utilisation of lesson time and the pace of pupils' learning. Differences in the overall scope and balance of topics did not seem significant; but there was some difference in the *order* in which topics are taught. In Switzerland physics courses are delayed till 14–16, when pupils' mathematical skills are expected to be sufficiently developed to permit teaching in some technical depth; in preceding years at Swiss schools pupils correspondingly spend more time on biology and chemistry.[54] In England, all science topics are taught throughout, often under an 'integrated approach' (combining physics, chemistry and biology); the advantages of integration, as a Swiss educationist put it to us on the basis of Swiss experience, are to be reaped more effectively at a later stage, after pupils have mastered the elements of the separate sciences.[55]

The IAEP survey analysed pupils' knowledge of science according to four main topics (life sciences, physical sciences, earth and space sciences, nature of science – that is, the nature of experimental methods) and three types of 'cognitive process' ('knows, uses, integrates'); under each head, average Swiss scores were ahead of English scores. In questions on physical sciences the gap was a little smaller, probably because of the delayed age in teaching physics in Switzerland. The gap was also a little smaller in questions on the 'nature of science', where the greater time spent on pupils' experimentation in English schools might be suspected of conferring an advantage; but, as said, Swiss average scores in both these respects remained ahead of English scores. In questions on 'using science', where it might also be thought that the English experimental approach would confer a considerable advantage, the Swiss were distinctly ahead.

Practical subjects

The difference between what is frequently termed the English 'academic bias' in schooling and the Swiss emphasis on preparation-for-life-and-work

---

[54] In more detail: for pupils in *Realschulen* and *Sekundarschulen*, physics is taken only in their final year, that is, at age 14–15; in *Gymnasien* the delay is till 15–16, though an introductory basic course (*Propädeutikum*) may be provided at 14.

[55] Despite a policy of 'integrated sciences' in most English schools, the difficulty of finding teachers competent in all three branches has been so great that, in practice, the physics component is often taught by a different teacher! Possibly this is a transitional difficulty, destined to disappear once a new generation of teachers has been trained; but as yet there is little sign of this happening.

(traceable to a continuing Pestalozzian influence) is manifest most clearly in the teaching at secondary schools of practical subjects such as woodwork, home economics or technical drawing. The greater need to take advantage of technological progress, and to provide higher levels of education particularly for pupils who previously went into low-skilled work, have led both countries – in, say, the past twenty years – to revise teaching in this broad area of the curriculum; but, despite the similarity of the technological pressures in the two countries, the gap between them in what is provided at schools in this area of the curriculum has widened significantly in this period.[56]

Until some twenty years ago the teaching of practical subjects in Britain and in Switzerland was recognisably similar: courses were offered in a variety of fields, such as woodwork, metalwork, home economics, textiles. Pupils were taught practical skills in these subject areas, and the objectives aimed at in British secondary schools were broadly comparable with those in Swiss schools; the emphasis was on achieving *high* standards in a limited range of materials (for example, metal or food, but rarely both). Courses on practical subjects were directed in both countries more particularly to pupils leaving school soon after the end of compulsory schooling.

In the past generation it has increasingly been thought desirable in Britain that practical subjects in some form should be taken by *all* pupils till the end of compulsory schooling. This raised the question, as it was put in 1967, whether practical subjects as traditionally taught could provide 'a sufficient intellectual challenge for the gifted pupil'.[57] Changes were progressively made to the way practical subjects were taught in Britain to suit what educationists thought were the needs of 'gifted' pupils. The changes culminated in the introduction of the National Curriculum for 'Technology' in 1990; this was a newly contrived and very broad subject, combining elements of Craft, Design and Technology (itself a combination, hardly ten years old, of earlier single-material subjects), home economics, art and design, and business education. The new provisions led to highly unsatisfactory classroom outcomes, as attested in reports from several sources

---

[56] The account given in this section draws on our previous comparisons of the teaching of practical subjects which included two further countries (Britain's industrial skills and the school-teaching of practical subjects: comparisons with Germany, the Netherlands and Switzerland, *National Institute Economic Review*, May 1993; and *Compare*, 1993, no. 3). The present version provides additional details on Switzerland and on more recent developments in Britain.

[57] Schools Council, *A School Approach to Technology* (drafted by D.I.R. Porter, HM Inspector of Schools), Curriculum Bulletin no. 2, London, HMSO, 1967, p. 13.

issued as from October 1991.[58] Public concern became sufficiently pressing by June 1992 for the Secretary of State to call for a revision of the Order. Proposals for a new Order were published in December 1992 and revised in May 1994 (by the School Curriculum and Assessment Authority under Sir Ron Dearing); a draft of a new Order was issued at the end of 1994 and incorporated in a revised National Curriculum in 1995.[59]

In Switzerland the teaching of practical subjects has also been extended in recent years to an increasing proportion of pupils. Until 1992 these subjects were taught in Zürich obligatorily in *Realschulen* (that is, schools for non-academic pupils) for three years at ages 13–15, and were available as optional subjects in *Sekundarschulen* for the final year at age 15; since 1992 they have been made compulsory for all pupils apart from those in *Gymnasien*. However, in contrast to Britain, the extension of practical subjects to a broader ability range was not accompanied by fundamental changes in the objectives of these subjects nor in the way they were taught.

On visiting a woodwork or metalwork class in Switzerland, pupils were usually found to be each working on an object to the same specification. The emphasis was on *making* real artefacts suitable for the capabilities of pupils in that class, and on finishing them to a high standard. The skilful use of tools was taught systematically: skills were demonstrated by the teacher to the class as a whole; pupils then applied and practised them by working on their project based on a specification or drawing provided by the teacher. The teacher checked pupils' progress at intervals to ensure that new skills had been absorbed properly, and he corrected malpractices.

Lessons in other practical subjects followed similar principles. For example, pupils in home economics classes prepared meals following recipes provided by the teacher; they also learnt about the dietetic and culinary properties of food. Having cooked the meal, they served and ate it – with due regard to table conventions. In textile classes Swiss pupils acquired practical skills in sewing, knitting and embroidery. At 13–14 they learnt

---

[58] A. Smithers and P. Robinson, *Technology in the National Curriculum: Getting it Right* (Engineering Council, May 1992); HMI, *Technology: Key Stages 1, 2 and 3* (June 1992); National Curriculum Council, *The Case for Revising the Order* (July 1992). These had been preceded by an initial report related to the present study from the National Institute team, S.J. Prais and E. Beadle, *Pre-vocational Schooling in Europe Today* (October 1991). For a selection of academic responses, see chs. 3 and 4 in the volume edited by J. Benyon and H. Mackay, *Technological Literacy and the Curriculum* (Falmer, London, 1992).

[59] *Technology for Ages 5 to 16 (1992)* (DfE, December 1992); *Design and Technology: Draft Proposals* (SCAA, May 1994).

to take measurements, make paper patterns, and produce simple items of clothing for themselves (for example, a zipped blouson); at 15 they worked from more complex commercially produced paper patterns. Swiss domestic sewing machines, with electronically controlled optional facilities, were used routinely.

In Britain, following the principles of the 1990 National Curriculum, pupils in their Technology classes were given a broad theme, such as 'marina' or 'celebration'; within such a theme they were required to produce their individual projects. The first step was to 'identify and state clearly needs and opportunities for design and technological activities through investigation'.[60] Pupils often spent many weeks – which might otherwise have been used for systematic teaching and making – in trying to decide on their projects; as HMI subsequently reported, 'pupils often spent too much unproductive time trying to identify needs; the outcomes were rarely satisfactory, and pupils sometimes become despondent about their lack of progress'.[61] For example, they observed that 'pupils in one school spent three weeks trying to identify a need associated with the theme of *communication*, but several became disillusioned and on week four brought in their own ingredients and made a pizza – a task which was quite unrelated to their earlier work'.[62] On our visits we observed 13–14-year-olds who, after weeks of brain-storming and research, ended in 'designing' and making some roughly finished wooden model boats and decorated Christmas cakes, as embodiments – respectively – of the two themes mentioned above, 'marina' and 'celebration'.

Once a 'need' had been identified and 'stated clearly', pupils were required to 'generate a design specification, ... produce a design proposal and develop it into a ... design'. Having worked on their artefact, they were required to 'develop ... an evaluation of the processes, products and effects of their design and technological activities'.[63] All this was required to be extensively documented in 'design folders'; the actual making of objects became marginalised. As HMI noted, 'in many schools insufficient time was allocated to manufacturing activities. For many pupils practical work was

---

[60] *Technology in the National Curriculum* (hereafter: NC Technology), HMSO, 1990. 'Identifying needs and opportunities' was specified as Attainment Target no. 1 in that document; the other three were 'generating a design', 'planning and making', and 'evaluating'.

[61] HMI Report, para. 16.

[62] *Ibid.* (our italics).

[63] NC Technology, pp. 7, 15.

Mini billiard table

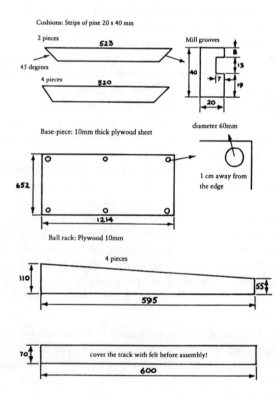

Frame:
Table top
18mm thick

160

Mill grooves:
11mm deep
11mm high
4cm from the
upper edge

632

Do not cut right through the long sides!

18

Side piece:

120
50

Use a fret-saw to make a hole (ball release)

It is worth putting a sliding door on the hole so that the balls do not fall out during play.

Cushions: Strips of pine 20 x 40 mm

2 pieces   523   Mill grooves

45 degrees

4 pieces   520

8
13
40   7   9
20

Base-piece: 10mm thick plywood sheet

diameter 60mm

652

1 cm away from
the edge

1214

Ball rack: Plywood 10mm

4 pieces

110   55

595

70   cover the track with felt before assembly!

600

Figure 2.1 *Example of woodwork carried out by 14-year-old Swiss pupils*

limited to activities involving light card and paper for model-making.'[64] The emphasis on written paperwork – that is, on documenting 'investigation', 'design', 'evaluation', and so on – also limited the complexity of pupils' practical projects to what each pupil was able to devise by himself. Academically weaker pupils who are not well suited to designing activities might have learnt to produce more complex products to high standards of quality if provided with specifications or drawings; such pupils were particularly disadvantaged by the requirement to spend much time and energy on their own design work.

The individualised approach to teaching in English schools encourages each pupil to make something different; moreover, pupils are to 'work at their own pace', and are thus mostly at very different stages. Consequently teachers can help pupils only on an individual basis; each pupil thus has limited contact time with the teacher and is mostly left to his own resources. In comparison with Switzerland, our observations consistently indicated that average and below-average pupils in England achieved much lower standards in their practical work than comparable pupils in Switzerland. In addition, their general motivation dwindled as a result of their inadequately structured learning experience and persistently disappointing rate of progress.

Swiss pupils generally made fairly straightforward but significant objects, graded according to their age, intended to be used by themselves or given away as presents, for example, decorated metal key rings, wooden boxes with sliding tops (made in the woodwork class, sometimes filled with assorted biscuits made in the home economics class), wooden blanket boxes (full-size, with metal hinges, carrying handles and locks), fashionable pieces of clothing. All were finished to high standards (for example, in woodwork, using successively finer grades of sandpaper; in needlework, starting with tacking stitches and finishing with embroidery stitching). The plans for a mini-billiard table shown in figure 2.1 give a not unfair impression of the kind of work done by average Swiss 14-year-olds (comparable plans for English classes are not relevant since each pupil is required to make his own individual design). Knowing that their objects were to be used provided Swiss pupils with an incentive to achieve a good quality of finish. The standard of complexity and finish of objects produced by 14–15-year-old Swiss *Realschule* pupils were judged by English craftwork teachers accompanying our visits to be generally comparable to higher grades (A–C) in the former single-craft subjects at CSE and O-level.

---

[64] HMI Report, para. 18.

When we were shown what English pupils had done as part of their practical work, teachers often proudly produced, not artefacts, but pupils' 'design folders'; this indicates the extent to which practical 'making' had become marginalised. The artefacts pupils produced – by those who reached that stage – were often a thing of the past as soon as they were finished, to be put in the classroom cupboard in case they needed to be assessed by GCSE moderators. The proportion of marks given to practical work at GCSE, as compared with 'design folder' work, was often under a fifth; English pupils were thus not provided with a strong incentive to achieve a high quality of finish. Exceptionally good examples of practical work were sometimes on display in the entrance halls of English schools – but these had usually been made by exceptionally good pupils, and cannot be taken as typical. Examples observed in classrooms by English pupils typically included much rough unfinished work, with levels of under-achievement never observed in Swiss classes. English children and their teachers no doubt often used their best efforts; but the tasks and curricular objectives in this area of schooling led to discouraging results.

Work habits

In addition to providing Swiss pupils with specific skills, practical subjects are regarded both by Swiss employers and by Swiss teachers as serving wider-ranging educational functions.[65] First, practical work is regarded as raising the standards of what is called *Arbeitscharakter* – which might be translated as 'general good work habits' – widely described as consisting of 'core skills' (*Schlüsselqualifikationen*) such as perseverance, reliability, care, patience, and precision. When employers select school-leavers as potential trainees these characteristics are often given equal weight with academic qualifications. Pupils from *Realschulen*, as a result of their

---

[65] The views expressed here on 'good work habits' attempt to summarise – primarily for the benefit of our English readers – what seem to us to be essential and important differences in attitudes towards practical subjects in schools in the two countries. We were particularly influenced by the differences in employers' views in the two countries. So much is widely taken for granted in Switzerland about the need to educate young people in school in 'good work habits' that they are often surprised that it is worth putting these matters into explicit words (for a fuller treatment, see Bierhoff and Prais, *op. cit.*, pp. 61–2). That Swiss schools put more emphasis on the 'formation of character', while German schools concentrated on 'instruction', was noted 150 years ago by Kay-Shuttleworth (v. fn. 2 above; and G. Howson, *A History of Mathematics Education in England*, Cambridge University Press, Cambridge, 1982, p. 107).

intensive schooling in practical subjects, are regarded by Swiss employers as having acquired particularly important advantages in respect of work habits which serve them well in mastering more complex tasks during their subsequent vocational training and at work.

Secondly, Swiss *Realschule* teachers regard practical subjects – in the way they are taught in Switzerland – as indispensable for many below-average pupils in keeping them motivated so that they persevere also with their academic studies. The sense of achievement that such pupils gain from their practical work, and the change in style of learning between academic and practical subjects, helps raise their general motivation at school. The levels of truancy of older pupils often found in English schools (especially inner-city schools) are unknown in Switzerland.

Thirdly, Swiss pupils acquire general skills relevant to subsequent employment: they learn how to be sensitive to suggestions for improvement in applied contexts, to put suggested improvements into practice, and to work at a pace appropriate to the task in hand. At British secondary schools, on the other hand, pupils are more often expected to 'discover for themselves', and 'work at their own pace'; the difficulty is that employers cannot afford such time-consuming methods in their training schemes. British school-leavers who go on to an apprenticeship thus often find difficulties in adapting to a way of learning and to a pace of activity for which they have not been well prepared at school.

Revised curriculum in England, 1994–5

The original objectives specified for the teaching of technology in Britain were broad and diffuse; they ranged from 'develop[ing] entrepreneurial skills in the youngest of children', and 'breaking down the academic and vocational divide [in] British education', to 'rekindl[ing] the huge creative power that characterised the first British industrial revolution'.[66] Indeed, so all-embracing were the original objectives that some originators of this new subject favoured a cross-curricular approach in which 'it would not be necessary to do any of the old craft subjects at all and ... technology could be delivered in history or geography, maths or science'.[67]

The expressed key concern of the Dearing Proposals for the revision of the National Curriculum in Technology issued in May 1994 was to

[66] D. Graham with D. Tytler, *A Lesson for Us All* (Routledge, London, 1993), pp. 53–4 (Graham was chairman and chief executive of the National Curriculum Council); J. Eggleston, Editorial, *Design and Technology Teaching* (1991, no. 3), p. 4.

[67] Graham and Tytler, *op. cit.*, p. 56.

'simplify and clarify the requirements of the [1990] Order';[68] there was no general intention to bring the requirements more into line with accepted curriculum practice in other countries. The new draft Order issued at the end of 1994 similarly did not question its original principles. It is however worth noticing that the Dearing *Proposals* wanted pupils to 'be taught ... to develop their *manual dexterity* and refine their *craft skills*'; this spark of hope was however soon quenched – no similar statements on manual dexterity and craft skills were to be found in the new *Order* when it was subsequently issued.[69]

Nevertheless, there has been an important relaxation for those schools wishing to follow a different approach. For 14–16-year-olds (Key Stage 4) it is now possible to fulfil the statutory requirements under the National Curriculum through a 'short course' (intended to absorb half of the time of a full course, say, 5 per cent of total curriculum time, or two school periods a week). In principle this should leave more school time available for practical work leading to an additional whole GCSE qualification in a single-craft subject (for example, metalwork). Such courses, and associated examinations, are to be developed by the GCSE boards (Wales, curiously enough, has been exempted entirely from NC requirements in technology at Key Stage 4); alternatively, a short course in technology might be combined with a short course in, say, metalcraft.

Though there have been other significant changes in the 1994 Order they will not be sufficient to bring English teaching practice in this field close to that of Switzerland (nor other Continental countries, such as the Netherlands and Germany). Under the previous Order very broad areas were to be covered by each pupil in the final two years of compulsory schooling; for example, pupils were required to work in at least three out of four categories of specified materials (textiles, graphic media, construction materials, food), and to work to four Attainment Targets ('identifying needs and opportunities', 'generating a design', 'planning and making', 'evaluating').[70] But, in addition to the wide range of more 'traditional' materials specified in the previous Order, under the new Order pupils are to be required to work with electrical and mechanical components, construction kits, control systems and structures; they are also required to 'investigate, disassemble and evaluate a wide range of products and applications to learn

[68] Draft Proposals, May 1994, p. iii.

[69] *Ibid.*, pp. 8, 12.

[70] The requirements varied: some NC documents required four types of material, others referred to a choice out of five – the fifth being 'information' (*sic!*); see the Appendix to our 1993 article (p. 69).

how they function'; and pupils' projects at Key Stage 4 'should require activity related to industrial practices and the application of systems and control'. The subject areas of the new Order are thus even broader than previously.[71]

Because of widespread criticism of the original four Attainment Targets, with their explicit emphasis on identifying needs and suggesting solutions, the number of Attainment Targets has been reduced under the new Order from the original four to two: 'designing' and 'making'. This alteration, however, is largely nominal. The 'making skills' to be acquired by pupils as envisaged under the new Order include a remarkably wide-ranging set of activities; for example: pupils should be taught 'to simulate production and assembly lines', 'how products are manufactured in quantity including the application of quality control and quality assurance', 'to produce and use detailed working schedules that will achieve the desired objectives, setting realistic deadlines for the various stages of manufacture, identifying critical points in the making process and providing alternatives to possible problems', 'to evaluate the quality of products and to devise modifications that would improve their performance', and so on. These ambitious objectives bear little resemblance to the modest down-to-earth way 'making' is understood in the teaching of practical subjects in Swiss secondary schools. In addition, pupils in England will continue to be required to 'generate ideas', 'identify appropriate sources of information', 'generate design proposals', 'develop ... design briefs and detailed specifications', 'devise ... test procedures to check the quality of their work', 'develop criteria for their design to guide thinking', and so on.[72] Many of the previous requirements are thus merely presented under different sub-headings in the new Order; and paper activities will continue to take up a great part of time in technology lessons.[73]

[71] 'One or more focus areas' are permitted under the new Order; but it has still to be clarified how this is to be implemented in practice (for example, can 90 per cent of the time be devoted to metalwork and 10 per cent to the remainder?).

[72] The arbitrariness of the NC allocation of tasks to the two Attainment Targets is evident from the overlap; for example, 'to be *flexible* in their working practices, in order to respond to changing circumstances and new opportunities' is listed as a Designing Skill, while 'to be *adaptable* in their working practices, in order to respond to changing circumstances and new opportunities' is listed as a Making Skill (see pp. 10–11 of the 1994 draft revised curriculum on *Design Technology*).

[73] After much effort and many resubmissions (and with the help of the Engineering Council, industry and schools), approval was eventually obtained in early 1996 for a GCSE engineering course under the new regulations covering design and technology in the National Curriculum; it is the closest in coverage of topics and

In Switzerland the topics to be covered by pupils in their practical work have also been increased in recent years – but by no means to the same extent. Under the curriculum introduced in Zürich in 1992, pupils irrespective of gender all carry out work in wood, metal, textiles and home economics in the first two years of secondary schooling, at ages 13–14; in the final year, at age 15, they are permitted to specialise.[74] There is now no division by gender in the choice of subjects as there had been in previous years. Standards of work in specialised areas appeared to our observers to have dropped somewhat since the broadening in the number of materials under the new curriculum. This may prove to be a disadvantage particularly for *Realschule* pupils; it is too early to say whether it will be outweighed by the benefits of a greater breadth of materials covered. Notwithstanding this change, Swiss lessons in practical subjects continue to be focused on the acquisition and refinement of practical craft skills in a way we have not observed in lessons in English schools.

Resumé and implications

This chapter has outlined how Swiss schools lead to distinctly higher attainments than British schools in three subject areas that are clearly relevant for very many pupils in their subsequent careers: mathematics, science and practical subjects (or 'technology'). The standards observed in these subjects in Switzerland were not in any way beyond those attained by *some* pupils in English schools; but significantly greater proportions of Swiss than

---

skills to the previous popular GCSE course known as *Engineering Workshop Theory and Practice* which was discontinued as not including sufficient design components under the new NC requirements. Coursework exercises to be carried out during the year cover similar topics (for example, *old*: make a hand-router; *new*: make a hole-punch for sheet aluminium). But there are two fundamental differences in weighting: (a) 20 per cent of total marks were devoted to coursework under the old scheme, but 60 per cent is required under the new scheme; (b) under the old scheme a further 40 per cent of total marks were allotted to a practical test to be completed in three hours (nothing corresponding to this timed task appears in the new scheme). We are indebted to Mr Nigel Sagar, General Inspector (Technology), London Borough of Barking and Dagenham, for advice on this comparison.

[74] As mentioned, *Gymnasien* are exempt from these requirements; what is said here thus applies to only about 90 per cent of all pupils. Additional voluntary classes were available in some schools we visited in pottery and photography. Technical drawing was obligatory for boys till 1992 throughout their three years at *Realschule*, but is now an optional subject available only in the third year.

English pupils reached good standards. Our classroom observations consistently confirmed the findings of the IAEP written tests of exceptionally good attainments by Swiss pupils in the lowest quarter or third of the attainment range; in mathematics, Swiss pupils in this section of the attainment range seemed to be ahead by a year or two even of average English pupils. This provided Swiss school-leavers with a much better foundation for skilled vocational training than available to corresponding school-leavers in England.

Some important common elements in the differences between the countries in teaching styles and syllabus content in these three subjects can perhaps be identified as follows. In mathematics there is no open-ended investigative work by pupils in Switzerland; in science, there is more demonstration by Swiss teachers of experiments related to basic scientific laws, and less time devoted to pupils' individual experimental investigations; in practical subjects, Swiss pupils spend almost all their lesson time each making something to a common given design, and very little time is devoted to individual designing. In Britain, on the other hand, individualistic 'investigative', 'discovery' and 'problem-solving' methods are all-pervasive, encouraging distinct work by each pupil: these methods are based on the notion that the teacher is to cooperate with individual pupils, or small groups of pupils, so that 'learning activities develop out of discussion between them'. In reality, with twenty to thirty children in a class, insufficient time is available for a teacher to deal adequately with pupils on a one-to-one basis, or even in small groups. Pupils in England are thus to a far greater extent left unguided and to their own resources, and too much of pupils' time is not spent effectively in learning.

In Switzerland, recognition of the need for pupils' active involvement in the learning process – which can be traced to the Swiss educationist Pestalozzi – is not lower than in England; but the way it is expressed in practice is very different. The Swiss teacher spends a considerably greater proportion of lesson time in *guiding* the learning of his pupils using a well-developed style of whole-class teaching with considerable question-and-answer interaction. The narrower range of attainment among pupils within each level of Swiss secondary schooling enables a Swiss teacher to fix on a realistic set of teaching objectives, and a suitable pace of teaching, to stimulate virtually all pupils in his class. While acknowledging the individuality of each child, the Swiss teacher builds to a greater extent on what pupils in the class have in common, and he works hard to take them forward together. The British approach, on the other hand, builds on existing differences among pupils and, in effect, enhances those differences; the teaching of an English class as a whole thus becomes increasingly difficult as pupils become older and the range of individual differences widens.

In short, a prime difference between the countries common to these three subjects, relates to the greater role in Switzerland of whole-class teaching. A second common difference can perhaps be identified in the greater Swiss emphasis on agreed basics – a basic mathematics literacy, a basic scientific literacy, and a proficiency in basic practical skills. In mathematics, for example, there is a greater concentration in Switzerland on basic arithmetic and areas; and in practical subjects there is greater emphasis on learning the use of tools and properties of materials within a specialised range (for example, woodwork). There is a wider acceptance in Switzerland that such basics need to be mastered by most pupils and need to be clearly expressed in the agreed curriculum; in Britain the National Curriculum documentation is broader and more imaginative (to put it at its best) – not only in technology which represents the extreme in these respects – but without managing to convey in any adequately understandable way the precise essential core of each subject.[75]

There is a noticeably greater evenness of Swiss pupils' attainments on entry to secondary schooling which results partly from the excellence of Swiss primary school teachers, and partly from the organisational mechanisms which support them. It would go beyond the aims of the present study to go in any depth into the distinctive features of Swiss primary schooling; but perhaps it is not out of place to mention here – since the same underlying principle governs their secondary schooling – that great attention is given to not putting a child into a class to which he is *not* suited. Swiss primary schools are based on mixed-ability teaching even more generally than in England; but the mix is limited by a greater reliance on the criterion: is the child 'ready for school'? This involves greater flexibility in ages on either side of a prescribed twelve-month range of birthdates than is followed in England, in order to ensure the child is ready in social, psychological and intellectual terms. Subsequent class repetition is consequently rare, and amounts to hardly more than one child a year per two

---

[75] Even in mathematics, a recent survey on the implementation of the National Curriculum reported that some mathematics teachers had 'difficulty in interpreting the statements [the syllabus requirements] into classroom practice. These statements are not just ones that are hard to give meaning to at a particular level, but are also statements that teachers do not understand.' Parents must have had even greater difficulties! See M. Brown, D. Johnson, M. Askew and A. Millet, *Evaluation of the Implementation of National Curriculum Mathematics at Key Stages 1, 2 and 3* (SCAA, 1993), Summary Report, p. 6.

classes; nevertheless, class repetition remains an ultimate sanction, and provides pupils, parents and teachers with a sense of immediacy and realism with regard to schooling attainments for which no counterpart is available in English schools.[76]

Finally, let us attempt – if only roughly – to assess the consequences of these overall differences in schooling attainments for the proportions of school-leavers ready for subsequent vocational training. Successful entry to craft apprenticeship courses in England generally requires that a school-leaver attains a pass at GCSE at least at grade D in three core subjects – English, mathematics and science (there is of course some variation; for example, a grade C in mathematics is usually required for more technical courses such as for electrical engineering craftsmen, while a grade E in that subject may be acceptable for building courses). Only the top 29 per cent of pupils in England were reported as having attained grade C or better in those three subjects in 1993; about another 10 per cent attained grade D, giving a potential total of some 40 per cent.[77] If the distributions of scores recorded by the IAEP surveys applied also at school-leaving ages, scores attained by the top 40 per cent in England would be attained by approximately the top 65–70 per cent in Switzerland; after creaming off the top pupils who prepare for university or other full-time higher education in both countries (say, 20 per cent in Switzerland, and up to 30 per cent now in England), we are left with barely 20 per cent in England who would be capable of entering a craft apprenticeship compared with 45–50 per cent in Switzerland. It is in this way that differences in secondary schooling attainments ultimately affect differences in the extent of a nation's vocational competence.

---

[76] A comparative study of the teaching of mathematics in primary schools in England and on the Continent, including Switzerland, is now in progress by the Institute in cooperation with the London Borough of Barking and Dagenham, and with the support of the Gatsby Charitable Foundation.

[77] DfE *Statistical Bulletin* 7/94, table 5, for A–C; estimates for grade D were interpolated from table 7.

3   Vocational guidance

The great Swiss educationist Pestalozzi spoke frequently of the teacher's duty to develop the 'head, heart and hand' of pupils in preparation for working life. The 'hand' element was intended to include such practical activities at school as weaving on a loom and working in the school garden; these activities would foster in pupils a 'spirit of industry', and thus help raise standards of knowledge and standards of living. An example of that broad view of the purposes of schooling is the memorandum he prepared dealing specifically with *The Combination of Vocational Training with Schools for the People*.[1] The emphasis given today in Swiss schooling to preparation for the world of work is thus of very long standing.

The greater role of practical subjects in the present-day Swiss secondary school curriculum has been described in the previous chapter; in the present chapter we move closer still to the needs of employment and describe what is provided in Swiss secondary schools by way of vocational guidance. As noted in chapter 1, vocational courses extending for 2–4 years are undertaken by some two thirds of all school-leavers in Switzerland – a greater proportion even than in Germany or any other European country; Swiss experience in guiding such a large proportion to vocational courses may thus be expected to provide contrasts with Britain worthy of detailed examination. The greater impetus and help given to Swiss pupils at secondary schools to look ahead at an early age, to overcome the urgencies and myopia of adolescence, and to prepare while at school for high-quality working

[1] Following extended correspondence in the 1780s, this memorandum was addressed by Pestalozzi to the Austrian Minister of State, Count Zinzendorf, in the hope of influencing policy there. It is remarkable how many of our present-day concerns for raising the educational standards of those whose employment is displaced by advances in technology were already evident then in the writings of Pestalozzi (see K. Silber, *Pestalozzi: The Man and His Work*, Routledge and Kegan Paul, London, 1960, esp. pp. 49, 71).

skills in as realistic a context as possible, are perhaps the predominating themes which will be recognised in the details described below. We shall consider in turn the differences between the two countries in: work experience as part of the final years of secondary schooling, the age at which vocational guidance is first given as a systematic course at school, the contents of such a course and related teaching material, styles of teaching, the role of the form teacher and the involvement of parents.[2]

Work experience

At least one week of 'work experience' is undertaken by the great majority of Swiss pupils, usually at age fifteen; it is widely recognised in Switzerland as the most important element of school-based vocational guidance in leading to a successful choice of career. Of course, most schools in Britain now also send their pupils on 1–2 weeks' work experience at age fifteen; but there are important differences in the nature of that experience. British pupils are expected to look on their period of work experience – not as preparation for apprenticeship, nor as preparation for a job with that employer – but are expected to pursue *highly general objectives*: to advance their 'general, personal and social development', their 'economic and industrial understanding', and to learn 'about the world of work'. They may be engaged in 'work shadowing', that is, watching others at work; or be given simple routine tasks, such as photocopying, filing, and so on. As the

[2] The preparation of the chapter has been helped by discussions with employers and educationists in both countries; we are especially grateful to Herr Albert Grimm, senior lecturer in vocational guidance in the (*Realschule*) teachers' seminary in Zürich, who also permitted us to observe final examinations of trainee teachers in this subject, and to Herr Bert Höhn of the Zürich central vocational guidance centre. A conference on Swiss vocational training, held in Bern in April 1992 with participants from neighbouring countries, provided a valuable account of current trends and problems (*Berufsbild in Umbruch*, Beiträge zur Berufsbildung Nr. 4, BIGA, EDMZ, Bern 1993; on the international perspective, see the article by J.-L. Chancerel, esp. p. 174). The account presented in the present chapter draws on the analysis of vocational guidance in four countries (Germany and the Netherlands, as well as Switzerland and Britain) in an associated study by Valerie Jarvis, Smoothing the transition to skilled employment, *National Institute Economic Review*, November 1994. For the sake of clarity it perhaps needs noting that our description in the present chapter of Swiss vocational guidance relates to the 90 per cent or so of all pupils in *Real-* and *Sekundarschulen*, and does not apply to the 10 per cent in *Gymnasien* who mostly proceed to university-level studies.

Department of Education's *Guide for Schools* (1991) put it: 'Work experience ... must *not* be seen as a specific preparation for, or means of entry to, any particular job or career: it should be designed always as a contribution to the general objectives [just mentioned]'.[3] Consequently, many pupils in Britain undertake work experience in occupations which they have no intention of entering in their later careers.

In Switzerland, in contrast, work experience while a pupil is still at school is directed to ensure as far as possible that the young person will embark on a specific traineeship with a specific employer suitable to his attainments, abilities and inclinations. It is usually preceded by an extended period of preparation at school to ensure that the best use is made of that week. In that period of preparation, pupils obtain details of a range of occupations, and the schooling requirements for entering them; and they are guided by a systematic process of assessment – including much self-assessment – as to whether different types of career match their abilities and inclinations. Preliminary half-day or whole-day visits by each pupil to several employers in the vicinity often help pupils gain closer insights into the suitability of careers that seem of interest; such preliminary visits are usually made to two or three prospective employers, but visits to half a dozen employers are not unusual (some of these preliminary visits may be undertaken as group visits, and may be preceded by a careers exhibition organised by local employers). The selection of suitable employers is aided by the local authority's career guidance department which compiles lists of trainee vacancies and helps schools in finding suitable placements.

While with an employer during the full week of work experience, the young person is often placed for part of the time alongside a trainee in the final year of his apprenticeship; the novitiate thus has the opportunity of realistically tasting what is likely to lie ahead during his apprenticeship. Equally, the employer has the opportunity of assessing the young person's suitability for such a career, and may have a set of standard tasks prepared for that purpose. The employer is interested not only in the youngster's schooling attainments and technical and physical capabilities, but also in his character: the extent to which the youngster 'critically checks his work ... his degree of patience, calmness, reliability, independence and persistence'.[4]

---

[3] *Education at Work: A Guide for Schools* (DES, London, 1991), paras. 7 and 13 (our emphasis).

[4] Further details are in *Real- und Oberschule bieten Chancen für die Zukunft* (Erziehungsdirektion des Kantons Zürich, 1982), esp. pp. 15–16 on *Schnupperlehre* – the Swiss term for trial apprenticeship; on the role of *Schnupperlehre* in

Subsequent discussions of pupils' work experience with the teacher in class, and among pupils, provide opportunities for reconsideration of career choice; these discussions are helped by a special diary with pre-printed headings (supplied to each pupil by the local authority's career guidance department) in which pupils note each day what they did, what they found interesting, difficult, and so on. Additional periods of work experience may be arranged to try alternative careers, or with other employers if the week with a first employer proved disappointing for either side. Work experience is often taken by all pupils in a class together in the same week; but it may also be undertaken during school holidays, and additional weeks can be taken by individual pupils during school term if necessary.[5] Work experience in Britain is normally arranged only during term time.

Age at which guidance begins

Vocational guidance at school begins in Switzerland, broadly speaking, when pupils are about a year younger than in England (reflecting, but only in part, the younger ending of compulsory schooling in Switzerland); the most substantial portion of guidance is provided in the school year prior to work experience, at about age fourteen. Some time is devoted to these matters in both countries also at earlier ages, and it is difficult to be very precise about the ages at which it may be said that vocational guidance really begins to take on greater significance. In the outcome, it is clear that by the age of fifteen when English pupils are still at the stage of being given only a generalised introduction to the world of work, Swiss pupils have each already formed fairly definite views on their own preferred career, and have gained a realistic understanding of what is required by way of schooling attainments to put their career plans into practice. Some not untypical examples: a Swiss 15-year-old wishing to become a mechanic will know what marks he needs to attain in specific subjects in his final school year in order to be considered eligible for an apprenticeship at a local engineering

---

promoting satisfactory career choice, see also U. Kraft, chapter Eiv in *Der Übergang von der Pflichtschule in das Berufsleben* (report of an OECD/CERI seminar, Salzburg 1985, Köllen Verlag, Bonn, 1986), esp. p. 127.

5 Up to one additional week for *Sekundarschüler*, two weeks for *Realschüler*, three weeks for *Oberschüler* – reflecting the greater difficulty the latter pupils may have in finding a suitable career (Beschluß des Erziehungsrates vom 23.7.1977, cf. A Grimm, *Berufswahlvorbereitung an der Real- und Oberschule*, Real- und Oberschullehrerseminar des Kantons Zürich, 1986, revd. 1992, p. 28).

firm; another wishing to become an electrician will recognise that he might do well to carry on voluntarily in full-time education for a year beyond the end of compulsory schooling so as to reach standards in physics and mathematics needed for electronic work. On the other hand, a pupil in England of that age whom we interviewed had undertaken work experience in some *unrelated* field (in accordance with the guidelines of the Department of Education, as mentioned above) and then decided to become a 'vet'; he was not untypical in not understanding the relevant qualification routes for his proposed career, nor that the science course he was taking at school ('single-subject science') and his likely school-leaving attainments had effectively precluded such a career.[6]

A significant fraction of pupils (a quarter is often mentioned) in British secondary schools show signs of losing motivation and interest in their studies in the last two years of compulsory schooling, say, at 14+. Unexplained absences – and persistent truancy by some pupils – become endemic. The Swiss schools selected for our visits deliberately included some with a fair proportion of pupils from problem families and from poorer areas; nevertheless, symptoms of demotivation among pupils at that age were conspicuously absent. No doubt many things are responsible for that difference, including the current higher employment in Britain – but also a different balance of schooling objectives: though career guidance may begin in Switzerland only *one* year earlier than in England, at that age the more detailed emphasis on specific careers may be a significant element in maintaining motivation. Moreover, the period of work experience helps to bring home to pupils the need for higher schooling attainments if they are to be accepted as trainees in their chosen careers.[7]

---

[6] While there is obviously much variability we believe the examples quoted above, from our team's interviews at schools in the two countries, give a quick but fair impression of the general contrast between the countries. Before the introduction of the National Curriculum and the associated official guidance (DES, *Education at Work, op. cit.*, 1991), some schools in Britain used the period of work experience to guide pupils towards a specific suitable career, much as described above for Switzerland; but that approach is now rare in Britain.

[7] These considerations apply more particularly to *Realschule* pupils. On closer analysis, some degree of demotivation is to be detected in some final-year classes at *Sekundarschulen* (as will be remembered, catering for middle-ability pupils) where many pupils have already been accepted for an apprenticeship early in the school year and feel that they can then 'lean back' (as it was put to us by a Swiss commentator). Some of the better pupils by that stage have also left *Sekundarschulen* to transfer to *Gymnasien* (or to intermediate full-time colleges, *Diplommittelschulen*, with a greater vocational emphasis), contributing to lower

Teaching style and differentiation

Careers education in England is treated as a school subject relevant to all pupils and is mostly taught in a 'mixed-ability' setting, that is, without differentiating pupils into separate groups according to academic aptitude or likely length of schooling relevant to their individual types of career. Pupils deciding whether they are more suited to work as hotel chambermaids or waitresses are thus taught in career guidance classes together with those deciding to become brain surgeons or research biologists; this situation obviously hinders meaningful class-wide discussion of alternatives. The task of the Swiss teacher is much eased by the streamed nature of their secondary schooling system, and the consequently narrower range of occupations relevant to each stream.

There are consequent differences between England and Switzerland in teaching style in careers lessons, similar to differences in other school subjects mentioned in the previous chapter. In England pupils are very much left to their own devices in making use of questionnaires, brochures, or interactive computer programs. In Switzerland each lesson is led by the teacher, and each lesson has its explicit aims. Much interactive discussion takes place between teacher and pupils in a whole-class setting; activities to be carried out by pupils individually, such as completing questionnaires, are preceded and followed by extensive class discussions.

Course content and teaching materials

Swiss schools have available pupils' textbooks on career guidance together with accompanying detailed teachers' guides, covering a systematic course for the three years of secondary schooling at ages 13–15. The most widely used material comprises a pupils' textbook of 88 pages (A4), which each pupil is expected to retain, an associated teachers' guide of 172 pages and a parents' brochure.[8] There seems to be nothing comparable in England, and it is therefore worth outlining the contents. About a quarter of the pupils' book consists of tests and structured questionnaires to clarify the pupil's interests and capabilities, and to match them with the

---

competition pressures in that final year; truancy was not seen as a significant problem even in these circumstances.

[8] E. Egloff, *Berufswahltagebuch* (for pupils), *Berufswahlvorbereitung* (for teachers), and *Elternrunde-Berufswahlkunde* (for parents), Lehrmittelverlag Aargau, Buchs, revd 1985 (these deserve translation into English).

characteristics of different occupations and different workplaces. The teacher's guide provides an exposition of the principles governing vocational choice, the didactic methods to be followed by the teacher, illustrative case studies requiring pupils to consider alternative decisions, and a suggested allocation of teaching material into a sequence of lessons ('teaching units') cross-referenced to the pupil's book. The teacher has freedom to choose whatever texts and teaching aids he finds helpful: nevertheless, this widely adopted textbook can be taken as indicative of what is usually covered in such courses.[9]

In more detail: at age 13–14 pupils' self-awareness of their comparative aptitudes is developed by guiding them to list their free-time activities and to reflect on why they enjoy them. A first parents' evening takes place at that age; suggestions for the organisation of such an evening are given in the teacher's manual. The next year, at age 14–15, covers the main part of the course. In the first half of that year, pupils' interests and aptitudes are examined in more detail with the help of structured questionnaires, beginning with questions such as: Do you enjoy reading and writing? How quickly do you become fatigued after mental or physical activity? Practical exercises are suggested to develop pupils' realistic self-understanding; for example, pupils are invited to carry out three physical exercises to assess their manual dexterity. On the basis of these assessments, pupils are guided to consider how their abilities and interests cast light on the type of career they would enjoy and in which they would succeed. Specific careers – both suitable and those better avoided – are listed for each pupil and considered in the second half of the year; 'dream occupations' (footballer, film actor) need to be understood by pupils as suitable only for those who are exceptionally gifted – and even such pupils are advised to prepare for a less ambitious reserve occupation. Local industrial specialisations are examined in detail. A range of some 25–30 related occupations often comes under discussion at this stage in relation to a typical young person's aptitudes and interests; but that number may be reduced in practice by local employment conditions, and is lower for those of limited schooling attainments.[10]

---

[9] See the chapter by A. Grimm in the OECD/CERI conference volume mentioned in fn. 4 above, pp. 109–20.

[10] The starting point for discussions with a pupil on suitable trainee occupations in Switzerland has so far been his interests, preferences and psychological aptitudes; the local availability of places has been taken as the second step in the process. Whether this ordering is optimal has been the subject of recent specialist debate, and may change following the shortage of trainee places that emerged in 1994. Swiss practice may thus move closer to that of Germany and Austria, where the availability of local (or regional) trainee places has generally been the starting point in career discussions in recent years. Shifts in the balance of supply and demand may promote a difference in current

In England a major part of career lessons is not uncommonly aimed at introducing pupils simply to broader aspects of the work environment – industrial relations, the implications of the international division of labour, the Single European Market – rather than, as in Switzerland, to guide pupils in their decisions towards a specific career. To help the latter decisions pre-printed questionnaires for completion by pupils are commonly used, but they are not as systematic nor as focused as in the Swiss material. For example, the main part of a widely used English questionnaire consists of a list of over a hundred activities, about half of which relate to occupations which normally require university graduate status or equivalent for entry; for each of these activities, pupils are asked to indicate simply whether or not they would like to carry them out: 'building an airstrip in a jungle or forest clearing', 'acting serious or comedy roles in films or on television', 'writing short "jingles" to advertise a product', 'being responsible for wildlife in a safari park', and 'helping school-leavers in choosing a career'.[11] The general lack of structure makes it difficult for a young person to evaluate their talents in relation to job requirements and to 'home in' on a suitable career.

As part of a Swiss pupil's career guidance lessons, and in preparation for spell(s) of work experience, initial interviews with local employers are held later in that school year (aged 14–15), preceded by practice interviews at school. Possible careers are then discussed with a careers counsellor by each pupil individually. Thus prepared, work experience is undertaken as described above; subsequent discussion with their teacher in class, and among pupils, provide opportunities for pupils to assess their work experience. They may then decide to apply for an apprenticeship with the employer with whom they undertook their week of work experience, or they may request another week of work experience with a different employer in that occupation or in a different occupation.

The final phase of the vocational guidance course deals with the nature of the agreement with an employer of a position as a trainee, and its legal and practical aspects.[12]

---

priorities in *discussions*, though of course in underlying terms both supply and demand always jointly influence the ultimate *outcome*.

[11] From the Occupational Interest Explorer developed by the Careers Research Advisory Centre (CRAC), (c. 1990, and still used in schools); the pupil marks 0 for 'no interest', 1 for 'not sure', 2 for 'I like it'.

[12] A summary of legal provisions to help pupils, parents and employers is also included at the end of the Zürich diary on *Schnupperlehre*.

The form teacher

The 'pastoral tutor' in English schools – sometimes the 'form teacher' (and sometimes both) – carry special responsibilities in advising pupils individ-ually on their careers, in conjunction with a specialist careers teacher and an advisor from the local employment department. Pastoral tutors and form teachers are assumed to be particularly capable of discharging this responsibility because of their greater opportunity to be in contact with 'their' pupils, and because of the resulting presumed better understanding of their pupils' capabilities and circumstances. There is however a fundamental difficulty. The predominant reliance in English secondary schools on specialist subject teachers has the consequence that the form teacher may teach 'his' pupils only one subject, and sometimes not even that (if the form teacher's subject is not taken by that pupil, the form teacher may do little more than take the attendance register in the morning and then not see the pupil till the next day).

In any event, he will not have the full and direct acquaintance with a pupil's comparative performance in a broad range of subjects that is characteristic of the Swiss form teacher. As explained in chapter 2, the form teacher in Swiss schools for middle-ability pupils (the *Sekundarschule*) teaches nearly half of all subjects – either humanities or sciences (usually only craft, and sometimes music and gymnastics are taught by subject specialists); in schools catering for less academic pupils (the *Realschule*) the form teacher has even more contact in that he teaches almost all subjects (usually only with some of the exceptions just mentioned). Further, a Swiss form teacher usually stays with his group of pupils throughout the three years they are in secondary school. The form teacher for the great majority of Swiss pupils thus has an incomparably fuller acquaintance with each pupil's relative strengths in different subjects and his personal characteristics and circumstances than his English nominal counterpart, and is thus in a better position to advise on alternative careers. This is a fundamental benefit to pupils, especially where parental support is deficient.

The broader ambit of Swiss teachers' responsibilities requires that their training course is correspondingly broader: how to provide vocational guidance to pupils thus forms an essential part of the training of all teachers for *Realschulen*. It requires trainee teachers to undergo a month of work experience with an employer who takes apprentices. During that month the trainee teacher observes in detail 'apprentice training, the associated attendance by apprentices at vocational college and the daily life of an apprentice'.[13] Trainee teachers take a final oral examination in vocational guidance, covering the didactics of vocational guidance, the characteristics of individual occupations, and the current local employment situation for school-leavers. The obligatory aspect of vocational guidance courses for *Realschule* teachers deserves careful notice since it is pupils in such schools – pupils in the lower part of the attainment range – who particularly need encouragement and guidance towards a well-chosen apprenticeship. In England, on the other hand, training in vocational guidance is not normally part of the requirements for a teacher's qualification.

Parental involvement

Parents in Switzerland are more closely involved throughout the process of their children's vocational guidance at school than in England. The underlying realities are probably these: first, the younger age of completion of compulsory full-time schooling in Switzerland (at 15+) contributes to a greater reliance by young persons on their family at the ages they receive vocational guidance at school; secondly, apprentice wages are so very much lower in Switzerland (as discussed in the next chapter) that financial support by parents normally continues in a more substantial way to later ages. The longer period of parental responsibility is embodied formally in the requirement that Swiss parents are signatories to the contract for their children's apprenticeship, together with the apprentice and the employer. Parents in Switzerland are consequently strongly solicited by schools to participate at all stages of their children's career choice.

In England, parental participation is encouraged as a general principle; but, in practice, it is marred by a degree of mistrust, and some schools do not even invite parents to individual career consultations.[14] Teachers suspect that parents are mistaken in tending to prefer their children to

---

[13] Grimm, *op. cit.* p. 111. The description here is based on Zürich *Realschule* teachers; broadly similar – but not identical – arrangements apply to other German-speaking Cantons. Teachers in other types of school may take optional courses in vocational guidance either as part of their training course (*Sekundarschule* teachers) or as supplementary training (other teachers).

[14] Cf. M. J. Taylor, Post-16 options: young people's awareness, attitudes, intentions and influences on their choice, *Research Papers in Education* (1992), vol. 7, pp. 332–4; T. Watts regards as 'questionable' the need to issue invitations for parental attendance at careers interviews (*Newscheck*, Department of Employment, May 1994, p. 13).

commence employment at sixteen, rather than stay on at school; while parents believe that teachers have limited knowledge of work opportunities outside school, and that teachers are improperly biased in encouraging pupils to stay on at school – since additional pupils directly boost the school's income. For many pupils in England who are not academically inclined, the final years of compulsory schooling all too often lack 'relevance'; and parents may not always be mistaken in thinking that in the two years after sixteen more could be learnt that would be of benefit later in life by taking on a job – however unpromising – than by staying on at school.

The ready availability of trainee and apprentice places in Switzerland, and the associated well-respected vocational courses and qualifications, makes the role of teachers, career counsellors and parents more straightforward and coherent when it comes to making proper provision for vocational guidance. Conversely, the underdevelopment of that route to an adult skilled career in England puts strains on all who have the responsibility for guiding the great majority of young persons – those who are not proposing to embark on university studies, but in reality are capable of much more than unskilled or semi-skilled work.

4 Vocational training and qualifications

Vocational training in Switzerland is voluntary: in that important respect it is like the English system – and unlike the systems of, say, Germany and the Netherlands which are founded on legally compulsory provisions for 16–18-year-olds.[1] Vocational training in Switzerland is also remarkable in that it has been undertaken to an increased extent in the past two decades, and today is undertaken by the majority of all young persons. Figures for Zürich may be taken as indicative: in 1978, 59 per cent of 20-year-olds had undertaken vocational training programmes mostly of three years' duration, rising to 72 per cent by 1991; that is to say, serious courses of vocational training and education were taken by an additional approximately 1 per cent of the age group in each year in that period.[2] In Britain, despite a series of important policy initiatives by the government in the past decade to encourage training, systematic vocational training to craft standards (City and Guilds part 2, or NVQ Level 3) remains low, and has probably declined in recent years as discussed in chapter 1. An examination of the detailed features of the Swiss training system should thus be of interest both from the point of view of understanding the main elements

---

[1] In brief: the German system usually requires *part*-time attendance at a vocational college for a day a week by school-leavers until eighteen (usually three years of attendance); one year's *full*-time attendance at a vocational college is usually permitted to be taken in substitution, but only a small minority of youngsters make use of the option. The Dutch system usually requires school-leavers to attend two days a week at sixteen, and one day a week at seventeen.

[2] Based on a detailed statistical analysis by S. Stutz-Delmore, *Schul und Berufswahl der Jugendlichen im Kanton Zürich* (Erziehungsdirektion, Zürich, 1992).

in its success, and from the point of view of possible policy implications for Britain.[3]

While primary and secondary schooling in Switzerland is governed locally – and varies to some extent among Cantons and even among school districts – Swiss vocational training and qualification procedures incorporate nationwide externally tested standards, mostly governed by Federal legislation.[4] Reliability, transferability and marketability are regarded as supremely important aspects of the Swiss vocational qualification process, and in these respects differ from the principles adopted in Britain when the reforms under its new National Council for Vocational Qualifications were introduced in 1986.[5] Common national *vocational standards* in Switzerland also exert a degree of pressure on secondary schools towards common *school-leaving standards* and help to moderate local variations in schooling.

This chapter begins by describing, and contrasting with Britain, the vocational training options available to young people in Switzerland and the associated vocational college courses; it then compares the standards aimed at in the two countries; finally, it considers costs of training and looks at emerging problems. While we shall exemplify from a range of occupations, greater attention will be given to engineering-related occupations because of particularly serious worries as to future supplies of such skills in Britain.

---

[3]   We are much indebted to Dr Escher and Dr Wettstein, of the Zürich vocational training department *(Amt für Berufsbildung)*, for kindly arranging visits to practical vocational examinations in Switzerland and for comments on an earlier draft of this chapter. In the final revision of this chapter we benefited from the latter's valuable survey, E. Wettstein, *Vocational and Technical Education in Switzerland* (DBK, Lucerne, 1994). We are also much indebted to employers in Switzerland and Britain for giving us access to their training sections and answering our questions.

[4]   Exceptionally, nationwide standards of training for health-related occupations have been delegated by the Cantons to the Swiss Red Cross rather than to the Federal authorities.

[5]   'We should just forget reliability altogether', was the view expressed by NCVQ's director of research in 1991 (see the discussion by S.J. Prais, Vocational qualifications in Britain and Europe: theory and practice, *National Institute Economic Review*, May 1991, especially fn. 4, p. 92). While it is arguable that this was said by way of rhetorical flourish ('surely, no responsible public servant in this field could mean that?'), it must at least be accepted – and unfortunately so from the point of view of young trainees in Britain – that reliability became very much a secondary consideration under NCVQ.

Main training occupations

Some 250 vocational qualification paths are officially recognised in Switzerland and cover virtually the whole ambit of the economy (for example, gardener, pastry cook, tailor, mason, mechanic, chemical laboratory assistant, secretary, dancer, ...); but that total gives an exaggerated impression of the effective number of training paths taken by school-leavers, since many qualifications are highly localised or highly specialised, and are followed by only a handful of candidates. It is instructive to list the most popular training occupations. For young men, half of all vocational qualifications awarded in Switzerland in 1991 were accounted for by just ten occupations: commercial work, electrical fitter, carpenter, electronics, car mechanic, machinery mechanic, construction drawing office, mason, plumber, salesperson. For young women, half of all vocational qualifications were accounted for by only three occupations: commercial work, salesperson and hairdressing.[6]

The issue of specialisation is in reality more complex. In all countries each training employer inevitably adds local elements of specialisation – implicitly or explicitly – to whatever the trainee is required to master for the purposes of attaining a nationally prescribed qualification. For example, a group of engineering firms (visited by our teams in the Zürich and Winterthur areas in 1992) developed a supplementary 'mechatronics' course, combining elements of mechanics and electronics, which is taken by all their apprentices pursuing nationally recognised qualifications for mechanical or electrical fitters; a pass in this supplementary course is noted by way of endorsement on their final certificates. To take another example: a salesperson may specialise, say, in ladies clothing or in foodstuffs. These supplementary elements approximately double the total number of distinguishable certificates; nevertheless the Swiss system attaches such priority to providing broad qualifications that the common core of examined subjects within each recognised training occupation accounts for some four

---

[6] Based on Swiss Federal Statistical Bureau publication no. 15, *Berufsausbildung 1991/92* (Bern, 1992). The greater breadth of female occupations that has emerged in the past two generations in Switzerland is well exemplified by the fall in dressmaking apprenticeships from 40 to under 5 per cent of all female apprenticeships in 1936–89, accompanied by a rise in female office work apprenticeships from under 10 to just over 30 per cent; the latter move displaced males from their predominant role in Swiss office work, falling from 80 per cent of all (male and female) apprentices to under half that percentage in that period (E. Ryter and K. Holenstein, ch. IIId in *The Swiss Educational Mosaic*, Federal Statistical Office, Bern, 1991, p. 58).

fifths of the final marks.[7] The core is often broader than might be imagined by an English reader; for example, the full *retailing* training course in Switzerland is sufficiently broad to permit someone with such a qualification to take up alternative *office work* requiring a grounding in bookkeeping, commercial correspondence, elements of law and office procedures. There is a significant contrast in this with the current approach in England under which many highly specific qualifications are distinguished – now proposed to be reduced to just under a thousand – in which qualifications have smaller central mandatory units. The Swiss aim is to provide an adaptable career-focused qualification, while England – in the present state of developing its structure of vocational qualifications – is content to certify occupationally specific competences.

In England, qualifications awarded at NVQ Level 3 are not yet sufficiently developed to permit an assessment of the degree of concentration of career choice at craft level since few qualifications have so far been awarded at that level (as noted in chapter 1). Figures for NVQ Level 2 (corresponding roughly to only the first year of a Continental apprenticeship) suggest the most popular courses are: business administration, business secretarial, business finance, hairdressing, retailing (engineering and building qualifications are *not* among the most popular!).[8] In Germany, the total number of vocational qualifications is similar to Switzerland's, but they are not quite as concentrated; the seventeen most popular occupations account for half of all male trainees, and nine occupations for half of all female trainees. The most popular occupations are similar to those in Switzerland, but with less emphasis on commercial work and more on engineering. Some of the apparent difference in concentration between Switzerland and Germany is to be traced to the fact that commercial qualifications in Switzerland are grouped under only two headings (*Kaufmännische* and *Büroangestellte*), while in Germany they are covered by some twenty more specialised qualifications, but with a considerable common base in the first two years of training.

[7] For example, the qualification for a retailing assistant gives a weight of 78 per cent to examinations in general educational subjects and general retailing, while 22 per cent is given to specific product-knowledge and practical selling skills in the particular branch of retailing in which the apprentice has trained (for example, ladies clothing). More strictly: a distinction can be drawn between the 'mechatronics' example, which is a local voluntary *addition* to the officially recognised qualification, and the specialised retaining knowledge which forms an essential *component* of the officially recognised qualification: the substance of the main point above is however not affected.

[8] *NVQ Monitor*, Winter 1993/94.

College courses

Vocational training courses in Switzerland vary in length (mainly) from two years, for example, for post office clerk and bus conductor; to four years, for example, for a car mechanic, electrical fitter, or drawing office technician. Courses of 3–4 years in length account for just over 70 per cent of all entering apprenticeships.[9]

A young person begins his apprenticeship by first entering into a training contract with an employer. He then becomes eligible to attend suitable college courses; indeed, it is an essential constituent of that contract that the trainee binds himself to attend vocational college during the full period of training, and that the employer will cooperate in making available the necessary time to do so. Attendance requirements vary from one day a week in workshop occupations such as building, to one and a half or two days a week in engineering and commercial occupations. In recent years (particularly since 1980) there have usually been three centres for each apprentice, namely, his college, his place of employment, and an industrial training workshop sponsored by local employers where he obtains *practice* on specialist equipment to supplement *demonstration* of equipment at vocational college (these arrangements are thus sometimes termed the 'triad system', in distinction to the previous 'dual system'; some occupations are exempted from this third type of centre). In principle, attendance at college is strictly enforced: a first unexcused absence from college (that is, without a doctor's certificate, to be countersigned by his training *Meister*) leads to a verbal warning, which is duly entered into his records; a second unexcused absence leads to a written warning and an 'administrative fee' of Sw.Fr 50–100 (equivalent to £25–50); a third occasion may lead to judicial proceedings with penalties![10] No doubt the last of these provisions needs rarely to be put into effect; but a legally enforceable ultimate sanction seems to be regarded in Switzerland as valuable to make it explicit that the rest of the

---

[9] One-year courses are now rare (domestic servants, air hostess, uniformed postman and telephone operator were included among one-year courses in the 1991/92 statistical summary on *Berufsausbildung*). A very basic form of training, '*Anlehren*', was created in 1980 for especially weak school-leavers, and is undertaken by about 1 per cent of all apprentices (Wettstein, *op.cit*, p. 29). In considering whether some Swiss courses might be unnecessarily 'long for the job', it should be remembered that they contain substantial general educational components (see next paragraph) and represent 'further education' in the wider sense in which colleges in England originally acquired that appellative.

[10] *Strafanzeige*; the details are from the Bern *Berufsschule* timetable (1991/92 edn, p. 2).

class must not be allowed to suffer because, for example, someone was away last week on an unexcused absence and now needs excessive attention by the teacher.

As indicated, the course of instruction at Swiss day-release colleges is considerably broader than might be expected by an English reader today, but not too different from German practice. The Swiss Federal *Reglements* relating to college courses detail the subjects to be taught, the number of hours to be given to each subject, the subjects to be examined, and methods of assessment. For most occupations about half the instruction time is devoted to occupationally specific subjects, and the remainder to general educational subjects (which 'are similar – but not identical – for all vocational courses). The latter usually cover language, mathematics, basic commercial organisation, economics, civics, gymnastics. The so-called occupationally related courses vary, but still include considerable elements that overlap with general education; for example, for an electrical fitter they include physics, chemistry, raw materials, technical drawing, electrical technology, domestic wiring. For retailing trainees there is more overlap: the occupational courses include product knowledge for the specific branch (dependent on local needs), sales techniques (greeting a customer, types of payment, delivery, and so on), shop management (range of merchandise to be stocked, purchasing, checking incoming goods, pricing, delivery, and so on), commercial correspondence, touch typing, window display; general subjects include arithmetic (emphasis on percentages, interest calculations on daily basis, mark-ups), local national language (taught as a broad cultural subject, as often in secondary schools in England, to include discussion of current events, the equable resolution of conflict situations, and so on), another national language (French, Italian), and gymnastics.[11] The general elements in these courses amount to an extension of the kind of education provided at secondary school, and are also seen as important in providing young persons with opportunities to discuss wider issues with a teacher independent of the trainee's place of work.

[11] The above curriculum for retailing is for the two-year course; trainees proceeding to the three-year retailing course (about a third of those completing the two-year course) also take bookkeeping, credit calculations (hire purchase, and so on), commercial law. The training and qualification requirements for each occupation are legally prescribed in *Reglements* (a booklet of c. 30pp.) issued by the Federal Ministry of Industry and Employment; the above details are taken from *Detailhandel (Erste Stufe: Verkäufer(in); Zweite Stufe: Detailhandelsangestellte(r))*, revd 24 November 1981. On education in the equable resolution of conflict situations, see also Appendix C below.

The contrast with requirements for vocational qualification in England is as black is to white: under the NCVQ approach there is no *requirement* for college attendance nor for external examinations; and written work is required only where writing forms an essential part of an occupation. Some employers in England nevertheless insist on attendance at college courses, though it forms no part of the new national requirements for a vocational qualification.[12]

Tests and comparative standards

With a broader ambit of studies for apprenticeship training in Switzerland, and a broader cross-section of the population attaining vocational qualifications, it must next be asked how standards compare in Switzerland and Britain (does more mean worse?). Comparisons of Britain's vocational standards with those of Germany some ten years ago by the National Institute of Economic and Social Research indicated that Britain's City and Guilds tests at part II were then broadly comparable with Germany's craft-level examinations (*Berufsabschluß*); this was reassuring, but perhaps not wholly surprising since in both countries these craft-level qualifications are usually awarded at age 19–20, after a three years' apprenticeship combined with day-release courses at college. Britain's problems at that stage thus did not lie with its vocational *standards*, but in the lower *proportion* of all young persons – usually well under half of Germany's proportion – aiming for and attaining vocational qualifications. That judgement was based on detailed comparisons with Germany of intermediate and final tests in

[12] The review of NVQs in 1995 (referred to again below, in chapter 5) carried out by Gordon Beaumont, who was previously personnel manager at several large companies, was specifically asked to consider whether 'knowledge and understanding' were given adequate attention in the original specification of NVQs. His report supported the original approach of NCVQ that 'knowledge and understanding should be integrated with performance in the workplace'; and no separate written examinations were recommended by him as a requirement, apart from a suggestion that 'separate assessment' might be 'appropriate' at higher levels. A further review of this issue in 1999 was suggested in his report in view of changes that had been recommended in January 1995 but which, it was thought, were too early to evaluate at the time of the Beaumont review (*Review of 100 NVQs and SVQs*, pp. 16–17; but surely some preliminary indication could have been attempted!). In reading that report it needs to be kept in mind that only a fifth of employers approached in the survey responded; the poor response rate was not disclosed in the printed report.

five major occupations: mechanic, electrician, construction worker, sales person, office worker.[13]

During visits to apprentice training departments in large engineering firms in Switzerland, standards of work by engineering apprentices were found particularly impressive by our teams. For example, a vertical drilling machine was required to be made by each apprentice during his four years' training at one of the engineering training workshops we visited; making all the components for such a machine was intended to equip these apprentices with the broad range of skills necessary for their careers: the machines were not otherwise required by their employer. The standard of workmanship (as judged by a British engineering graduate in our team) was far above that expected of craft apprentices in Britain, and close to that expected of students following a British university degree course in mechanical engineering.

When we compared Swiss final *written* examinations for the same five occupations mentioned above (in relation to our comparisons with Germany) we found standards broadly similar to those of Germany, and perhaps a little higher. In addition, our teams observed final *oral* tests and *practical* tests administered to individual apprentices who had trained as: precision mechanics, electricians (domestic installation work), salesperson (specialising in ladies clothing), and two types of office work (travel agent, personnel and accounts office). These oral and practical tests supplemented their written examinations and went into remarkable depth related to the particular experience of each candidate during his apprenticeship.

By way of example, we may outline the main features of the final *practical* tests for engineering apprentices. These consisted of two substantial tasks. First, a ten-hour task, requiring a variety of basic machining operations, was taken by all machine fitters irrespective of their specialisation: this was judged by British evaluators to be broadly comparable in *range* of operations to that expected at the end of their third year by British apprentice fitters, but the degree of *finish* specified (chamfers, tapers, and so on) was significantly higher, and would be attainable by only about the top quarter of British apprentices; the basic Swiss standards might thus be described as attainable by those who in Britain enter *technician* rather than *craft* apprenticeship courses. A second task, specified to last fourteen hours, varied according to line of specialisation; an example for precision engineering fitters is shown in figure 4.1. This task is difficult to complete in

---

[13] S.J. Prais and K. Wagner, Some practical aspects of human capital investment: training standards in five occupations in Britain and Germany, *National Institute Economic Review*, August 1983.

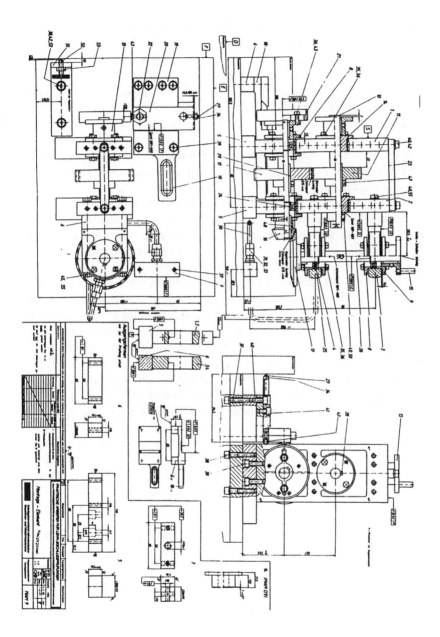

Figure 4.1 *Example of a 14-hour practical test for Swiss precision engineering fitters at the end of their apprenticeship*

the required time; penalty marks, laid down in detail by the Federal authorities, are to be deducted for overrunning and for imperfections (taking into account the accuracy of the artefact within prescribed tolerances, the speeds at which cutting tools were used, any remakes of parts made badly on a first attempt, cleanliness and orderliness of the working area, and so on). About half the candidates are able to complete the task in the prescribed time and another third overrun by half an hour; overrunning by three hours almost certainly means failure. However, of those who enter this examination, only a negligible number fail. English evaluators again doubted whether any but the very best of English apprentices would be capable of completing this task in the assigned time.[14]

The requirement to complete an extensive and complex task within a tight time limit puts realistic pressures on a Swiss candidate of the kind familiar in commercial practice. He has to decide how far to go in pursuing perfection in each of the varied constituent tasks that confront him: he has to balance a modicum of imperfection (to 'cut some corners') in less important aspects and lose only a few points, against more points to be gained by finishing on time. The course and examinations have to be completed successfully within the specified normal number of years, and only one attempt at a repeated examination is permitted. There is a significant contrast in all this with the English NCVQ's principles under which no rigid time limits are specified for any particular learning process or training syllabus; a task may be attempted several times virtually without penalty, and its eventual successful completion is sufficient for it to be 'ticked off'.

Practical and oral final examinations observed by our teams in other occupations in Switzerland were correspondingly impressive. It would overburden this chapter with detail to report more than one further example, namely, practical and oral tests in retailing – an occupation in which training in Britain is undertaken mostly at only a very basic level, and training at craft level (NVQ 3) is a rarity.[15] The candidate we observed being

---

[14] British evaluators included experts from the Engineering Industry Trade Board, the Engineering Council, and heads of engineering departments at colleges of technology. Corresponding British tasks were shown to experts abroad. There was a remarkable degree of conformity in the assessments from these different sources. German practical tests were judged closer in difficulty to those set as the first Swiss task (the ten-hour project); this provides an indication of the somewhat higher standards aimed for in Switzerland (but further comparisons would be necessary if this issue were to be of policy significance).

[15] V. Jarvis and S.J. Prais, Two nations of shopkeepers: training for retailing in France and Britain, *National Institute Economic Review*, May 1989, p. 63 and n. 27.

examined had served her apprenticeship in the women's clothing department of a large store. The first half-hour – the practical part of the test – was spent on an actual shopfloor, while real customers were circulating normally in the shop; the trainee was engaged in intensive 'selling' of a range of clothing to an examiner who acted as a customer about to go on holiday. For the second half-hour, the oral part of the test, the examining group moved to a private room where some eighty garments were on a rack; the examiner took out in turn some two dozen varied garments, spending about a minute on each, and questioned the candidate on quality details. For example, material content had to be identified by the candidate (without looking at the label); characteristics of three types of wool were listed by the candidate according to type of sheep and their geographical origin, and the main stages in the processing of wool from sheep to customer; suitability of materials for different purposes (keeping warm, dry, wrinkle-free, and so on); methods of cleaning the garment (how should crushed crepe be washed?); names of typical fashion styles (Chanel costume, Raglan sleeves). No doubt similar standards of knowledge may be encountered in English shops, but only rarely today since product knowledge – if required at all – is no longer given importance in training for our retailing qualifications.[16]

Taken as a whole, five aspects of these comparisons seem worth emphasising from the point of view of current debates in Britain. First, there can be no doubt that a very much greater proportion of young persons in Switzerland than in England reach very high *vocational standards* (in this case, 'more does not mean worse'); the international success of, for example, the Swiss precision engineering industry is thus seen to be based on a broader and firmer rockbed of highly skilled personnel than is available in Britain. Secondly, the *age* at which that greater proportion attains those higher skill standards (about twenty) is no higher than for craft-level qualifications in England; the case for extending the average length of full-time education

---

[16] Further details of the organisation of oral examinations in Switzerland are available in a 100pp. report by C. Metzger, *Mündliche Prüfungen im Fach 'Praktische Arbeiten/Kenntnisse aus Lehrbetrieb und Branche'* (Institut für Wirtschaftspädagogik, St Gallen, 1992). For example, it advises that a team of expert examiners should examine no more than twelve candidates a day (p. 41); the layout of the room is prescribed, including the seating arrangements for guest observers (p. 43) – which was followed precisely on our visits; and it provides a specimen report to be drawn up by an employer on a trainee's experience to assist the examiners in detailing questions for the oral tests (p. 36). How best to examine commercial qualifications is discussed in *practical* detail in a further recent (1994) report from that Institute by C. Metzger and R. Waibel, *Sind die kaufmännischen Lehrabschlußprüfungen gültig?*

in England needs therefore to be questioned. Compulsory full-time schooling ends at 15+ in Switzerland, compared with 16+ in England, though often an extra year in Switzerland is now dedicated to full-time pre-vocational education or is otherwise spent as a 'gap year'.[17] Thirdly, the breadth of *general education* which forms an obligatory part of vocational Swiss day-release courses helps offset any worries that these young people – with their shorter period of compulsory full-time schooling – are undereducated in general educational subjects when compared with their English counterparts. Indeed, our interviews with trainees elicited a coherence and clarity of response matched only rarely in England. Fourthly, the *slice of the attainment range* from which most Swiss mechanical engineering apprentices are drawn can be said to be roughly the middle third of school-leavers; most of the corresponding slice of English school-leavers – though staying compulsorily in school till they are a year older – would not be sufficiently prepared in mathematics, nor in practical subjects (and technical drawing), to enter a course at standards current in Switzerland. High and relevant school-leaving standards are thus a precondition for high-level vocational training.[18] Fifthly, as was repeatedly mentioned to our observers, Swiss vocational qualifications are concerned to certify not simply that the candidate has correctly carried out a specified set of tasks or produced a specified set of components; rather, the apprentice's *training is oriented towards a progressive career*, and the combination of written, practical and oral tests is intended to permit candidates to display independence and promise of advancement in a distinctly broader way than conceived under NVQs in Britain.

A final general issue, that perhaps still needs emphasising in Britain, is the overriding attention given in Switzerland to ensuring the trustworthiness of qualifications. In Britain under NCVQ, the assessment of a candidate takes place as far as possible in his normal workplace by his normal supervisor under normal working conditions. There is a proper place for this approach; but the Swiss approach – as on the Continent generally – is that, while 'the most important part of the practical training involves

---

[17] Average age of entry to an apprenticeship has recently been about sixteen and a half.

[18] See chapter 2 above. Swiss engineering employers spoke in terms of their apprentice intake ranging from the top half of *Realschule* leavers to above-average *Sekundarschule* leavers. Where there was much electronics and automation, average to above-average *Sekundarschule* leavers were sought by employers; on the other hand, the majority of apprentices for mechanical fitters, even in precision engineering, still came from *Realschulen* at the time of our visits.

participation in the ordinary business of the enterprise', when it comes to certifying a qualification it is essential to provide for external independent and objective assessment.[19] For that reason it is required that tests must *not* be carried out in the workplace in which the apprentice received his training, that national written tests form a substantial part of the total assessment, and that none of the examiners and consultant experts may be acquainted with the candidate in any way. These safeguards serve to ensure that the certificate of qualification carries national credibility.

As we learnt from employers we visited in Britain, since there is now (following NCVQ reforms) no longer any requirement for attendance at college nor any central written examinations, there is much greater variability in what might be learnt during an apprenticeship. Consequently, an employer more often than previously, and perhaps now in the majority of cases, finds he cannot rely on the meaning of an NVQ if a recruit has been trained at another company, and has virtually to reassess him. In other words, the formal certification procedures under NCVQ do not provide that transferability and marketability of skills which form such vital elements of the benefits of organised qualification procedures, and help justify their costs.

Costs of training

The costs of the more extensive training that young people receive in Switzerland are carried by them to a greater extent than in Britain, in that they receive a remarkably low wage or trainee allowance. During the four years of a Swiss engineering apprenticeship, for example, trainee allowances in 1993 averaged only 24 per cent of the earnings of a newly qualified craftsman (rising from 16 per cent in the first year, to 20, 26 and 34 per cent in the subsequent three years), with sometimes a small bonus varying according to a trainee's achievements. Trainee wages in Britain in the same year were over twice as high, at about 62 per cent of adult skilled craft rates (rising during four years of an apprenticeship from 44 to 55, 67 and 83 per cent). Immediately after qualification, a Swiss engineering craftsman may earn little more than an unqualified operative of the same age who has spent the intervening years entirely in gaining experience; but after ten

[19] A. Borkowsky, ch. 111a in *Swiss Educational Mosaic* (*op. cit.*), p. 40.

years a qualified craftsman will be earning some 50 per cent more than an unqualified operative.[20] The main gap in lifetime earnings in Switzerland is now not so much between the various grades of qualified persons, but between those who are unqualified and those who have attained a vocational or higher qualification.[21] Social approbation of the qualified craftsman in Switzerland substantially reinforces financial incentives to undertake training; those who remain vocationally unqualified (*'ungelernt'* – carrying a connotation of uneducated) – whether because they have not undertaken or not completed an apprenticeship – are classed in popular Swiss opinion today among the 'marginalised groups of society'.

In Britain skill differentials have been much compressed since the 1970s, and have begun rising again only in the past decade; for example, the differential between fitters and operatives in metalworking occupations, as recorded in the New Earnings Survey conducted by the Department of Employment, was of the order of only 15 per cent in the mid-1970s, rising

---

[20] The figures on Swiss earnings are based on an unpublished compilation of trainee allowances of fourteen large engineering firms in the Lucerne area and on our interviews. Trainee bonuses in a large engineering firm that we visited varied according to a trainee's assessed success as follows: 5 per cent received no bonus, just under half of all trainees received an 18 per cent bonus over basic rates, and just over half received a 28 per cent bonus. Assessments of success are made quarterly under the headings of 'diligence, attainment, behaviour, reliability and record keeping' (see the report by H. Oelz and C. Aeberli in *Lernarbeitschaft und Lernfähigkeit zwischen Schule und Beruf*, ed. J.-P. Meylan, Köllen Verlag, Bonn 1988, p. 168). The previous National Institute study by H. Hollenstein (*Economic Performance and the Vocational Qualifications of the Swiss Labour Force compared with Britain and Germany*, NIESR Discussion Paper No. 54, September 1982, p. 42), comparing Britain and Switzerland some ten years ago, reported average Swiss trainee allowances at 17 per cent of the '*average* earnings of skilled manual workers (male)'; this is not inconsistent with the proportion of the earnings of a *newly qualified* craftsman quoted here.

[21] From a careful analysis of a sample study of incomes and qualifications (carried out in Geneva in 1991 by the Swiss Vocational Office, BIGA, and the Geneva Statistical Office), it appears that there was little difference in the lifetime discounted earnings of university graduates, *Meister*, and commercial college graduates, who earned some 28 per cent more than an unqualified person, while someone with a vocational qualification earned 18 per cent more than an unqualified person. The latter gap thus appeared as the most significant to the analyst (see S.C. Wolter, Lohnt sich Bildung überhaupt?, *Economic Focus* (UBS/SBG, Zürich), September 1994, pp. 1–8, esp. graph 4).

to 21 per cent in 1987, and had recovered to 37 per cent by 1993.[22] Regrettably the Department's survey does not distinguish between those who are formally *qualified* as fitters, and those who are *employed* to carry out such tasks solely on the basis of their experience; these figures are however consistent with the simple interpretation that higher differential rewards for vocational skills in Switzerland have provided greater incentives for youngsters to undertake vocational training, despite receiving lower allowances during their training period. At the same time, lower costs of training have provided Swiss employers with a greater incentive to employ trainees and to provide them with a first-class training.

That simple interpretation may be realistic for most occupations, where no very highly expensive equipment is involved. But in much of large-scale modern engineering, costs of training have risen immensely; net costs equivalent to £5–10,000 a year per apprentice are now often mentioned by the largest firms in both countries. Even allowing for employers' possible underestimation of the contribution to production by an apprentice (a frequent problem in such costings), it is not too difficult to understand why the viability of parts of the training system have come under question – even in a country where training has been as widespread and as successful, and trainee allowances as low, as in Switzerland. The contributory factors to increased training costs seem to be these. In modern large-scale engineering, automated and linked lines of expensive machinery are often involved; in such conditions there are fewer small jobs of the kind that used to be delegated to a trainee and which helped 'pay for his keep'. There is also a greater risk of substantial loss if the trainee makes some quite small error while looking after a section of the line. Consequently, extended periods of off-the-job training have been introduced to allow apprentices to acquire the more complex theoretical concepts and skills to operate modern production equipment; this is expensive in itself, and there is negligible offsetting marketable production by trainees.

[22] These figures for Britain are taken from the *New Earnings Survey 1993*, Part D (table 86), and relate to metalworking production and maintenance fitters as compared with metalworking operatives on press stamping and automatic machines. For an earlier longer-term survey of trends in skill differentials in Britain (with slight changes in definitions in earlier years), see S.J. Prais, Productivity and management: the training of foremen in Britain and Germany, *National Institute Economic Review*, February 1988, p. 40. Information on craft apprentices' wages, based on averages of five large engineering firms was reported in IDS Study 534, *Young Workers' Pay* (London, July 1993; the five firms were: Jaguar, British Aerospace, Nestlé, Bonas Machine, Holset Engineering).

Not surprisingly, in such industries it is now often said that even the very low trainee allowances characteristic of the Swiss training system are no longer sufficiently low to make the provision of 'in-house' training worthwhile to employers. Till very recently those low allowances ensured adequate apprentice places and subsequent employment for qualified youngsters: 'There is virtually no youth unemployment in Switzerland', reported an OECD *Review* team in 1990. That *Review* contrasted the successful Swiss system of market 'interaction of supply and demand' for work-based apprenticeship places with the system of full-time vocational colleges which have increasingly replaced apprenticeships in France in the past decade, and the accompanying immense youth unemployment there. The numbers for each occupation trained there in full-time colleges have increasingly been determined by educational planners, and their judgement must come under question as not having been as successful as the market mechanism in anticipating shifts in supply and demand.[23] Economists have frequently noted that labour markets adjust only slowly to underlying changes; that is to say, as supply and demand conditions for products of different industries or of different countries change, there are only slow changes in relative wage levels and in the consequent flows of employees required from contracting to expanding industries. Similarly, in the case of the apprentice market, trainee allowances tend to be rigid over long periods, and symptoms of excess supply or demand for trainees manifest themselves. On our more recent visits to Switzerland in 1994 (four years after that OECD report) the world economic depression was widely said to have contributed to an overall decline in the availability and choice of trainee places to an extent not previously experienced there. Large engineering firms which we visited continued to invest in trainees, but in a moderated way. Often training was carried out not solely with a view to providing adequate future qualified personnel for themselves, and it was expected that many trainees would not be offered employment by their 'training firms' after qualifying. Large firms sometimes spoke of training activities as a form of voluntary service to the economy and to society as a whole. Smaller firms (especially in craftwork) continued to provide sufficient training places to absorb

---

[23] OECD, *Review of National Policies for Education: Switzerland* (Paris: German version and summary in English, 1990; French and full English versions, 1991); the quotations are from the English summary, p. 21. The issue deserves fuller study; it is obviously too simple to attribute France's youth unemployment solely to the shift from apprenticeship to full-time vocational colleges; on the other hand, it would be equally too simple to disregard that shift as a contributor to their current problems.

current flows of school-leavers, though not necessarily in the kind of occupation that youngsters preferred; more youngsters than previously took an extra year of full-time pre-vocational schooling in the hope of finding a training place next year closer to their ambitions.

The Swiss apprenticeship system, while continuing to function satisfactorily on the whole, was thus in 1994 beginning to express incipient symptoms of malfunctioning similar to those that have for long been more seriously evident in Britain. In technically complex occupations there is now a greater tendency for employers to look for higher school-leaving standards, and to encourage apprentices to receive two days (instead of one, or one and a half days) a week release from work for attendance at college to reach higher vocational standards.[24] While changes have to be made in both countries' training systems in response to the needs of more complex technology and competition from low-wage countries, Switzerland clearly starts from a much higher level of vocational attainments in planning its reforms. The main features of those reforms will be discussed at the end of the final chapter.

[24] Wide-ranging discussions of possible changes in the Swiss training system are to be found in the conference volume *Berufsbildung in Umbruch* (BIGA, Bern, 1993), especially the paper by Professor R. Dubs, pp. 71–89, and the discussion on pp. 246–8.

5   Problems and developments

How to cope with the current threat of prolonged unemployment – recently especially high among the young and unskilled – and how to ensure that best use is made of automated methods of production and modern technology, are issues of the greatest seriousness in all advanced industrialised countries today. We have seen in previous chapters that Britain and Switzerland – both advanced industrialised economies from a global perspective – have developed over many decades different frameworks for their skills training, different mixes of schooling objectives and, more generally, different ways of helping youngsters in their transition from school to work. The task of this final chapter is to outline and compare recent changes in those frameworks, and to consider what lessons they may provide for future policies (some of the main points of earlier chapters are repeated here for convenience of exposition).

Technology, trade and unemployment

Let us set out the underlying developments in a little more detail. The progress of technological innovation is worldwide, with great variation in rates of progress: some countries are substantially ahead of others, some are catching up, others are overtaking. Countries where wages have been relatively low learn to produce goods previously beyond their capabilities, export them to countries which so far have been industrial leaders, and displace those employed previously in those branches. Easier transport and communication between countries have encouraged greater international trade, the reaping of greater economies of scale, and greater international specialisation. Absolute and relative wages of the skilled and unskilled consequently have changed both in industrialised and in developing countries; substantial readjustments in international specialisation have consequently taken place in recent years, and seem likely to continue for many decades to come.[1]

A twofold educational task now clearly falls on industrially advanced countries. First, they need to ensure that the technological capabilities of their scientists, engineers and technicians are adequate to be able to apply new processes rapidly from whichever part of the world they originate, to take part in the further development of those new processes, and to be among world leaders in at least some fields of specialised innovation. Secondly, advanced countries need to make new provision for that substantial part of the workforce who in previous generations carried out simpler, repetitive, unskilled or semi-skilled tasks, and had been provided with basic education more or less acceptable and efficient for that purpose – but which is now inadequate for the pace of readjustment brought about by the global advance of technology and increased foreign competition. In relation to that second task, Alfred Marshall's dictum of over seventy years ago applies now even more strongly:

> The aim of social endeavour must be to increase the numbers of those who are capable of the more difficult work of the world, and to diminish the numbers of those who can do only unintelligent work, or who perhaps cannot even do that.[2]

There is thus now a modern urgency to improve education and practical competence at both ends of the spectrum of human ability. But which end is more important? It might be thought we need not worry too much: that it continues to be adequate to urge that more resources be devoted to education generally – virtually as if we were dealing with a one-dimensional substance, the precise composition of which was a detailed matter of no great consequence. That is often the approach of many expert economists

---

[1] For a valuable short theoretical introduction to the changing international location of manufactures according to their stage in the product cycle (new, maturing, standardised) an article published in 1966 by R. Vernon can still usefully be consulted: International investment and international trade in the product cycle, *Quarterly Journal of Economics*, 80, 190.

[2] Opening of the final paragraph of his *Money, Credit & Commerce* (Macmillan, 1923), p. 263.

and educationists when they write about policy matters.[3] But with continued high levels of unemployment in advanced industrialised economies, the need grows to discern, identify, and give greater attention to those educational policies that bear on the reduction of unemployment, more especially among the young and unskilled. Apart from the obvious immediate loss of output associated with unemployment, and the tax burden placed on those in employment to finance welfare payments to those who have not succeeded in gaining employment, there are long-term consequences of *individual* demotivation, misery and degradation and, ultimately, wider consequences of *social* divisiveness leading to increased crime and, perhaps eventually, to political instability. We need therefore consider critically here the differences between recent British educational policies which have been particularly effective, for example, in increasing numbers of university graduates; and Swiss educational policies, which have been more effective in providing the great majority of the workforce with high educational attainments, and yielding lower unemployment.

Higher education

The rapid increase in the past decade in Britain's proportion of school-leavers entering university courses – now 30 per cent of each age group,

---

[3] A. Wood (*North-South Trade, Employment and Inequality*, Clarendon, Oxford, 1994, esp. pp. 355–65) emphasised that the recent growth of unemployment in advanced countries is to be seen largely as a response to changes in the international division of labour based on differing skill endowments. He commends the UK's 'expansion of university student numbers, introduction of a national school curriculum, and more training for the unemployed' (p. 355); but, perhaps because he writes as a general economist concerned with foreign trade, he does not attempt a critical appraisal of the effectiveness of those educational policy moves. (There is an unfortunate interdisciplinary gap: just as economists tend to avoid analysing the economic requirements for educational reform in detail, so educationists avoid analysing their proposed reforms of the educational system in relation to the changing detail of the economy's requirements.) The dispute among certain economists as to whether the primary driving force behind current unemployment in Northern counties is *technology* (for example, automation displacing unskilled repetitive labour) or increased ease of *trade* with Southern countries (for example, imports of labour-intensive products from low-wage countries) need not concern us, since their proposed remedy is usually the same – better education and training. The imposition of trade barriers as a remedy is not regarded by anyone as providing a satisfactory long-term solution.

with a rise to 40 per cent under discussion – is the clearest indicator of Britain's continuing emphasis on top academic qualifications. This policy is broadly in line with the US pattern, despite worries aroused by the large number of under-achievers ('drop-outs') there, and without regard to the greater extent that American students undertake part-time employment to finance their university studies and the greater occupational focus of their studies. There is a clear contrast to Switzerland's mere 11 per cent of each age group who have graduated from universities in recent years; increases under discussion there are only to the order of 15 per cent.

While in both Britain and Switzerland there has been a nominal (credentialistic) element in recent increases in university numbers, the real accompaniments are not unimportant, though some of the benefits are debatable. In Britain, colleges of technology, institutes of higher education and polytechnics – which previously had substantial specialisations in technical and vocational studies with much provision for part-time students who combined work with study – have been progressively raised in 'status'; many were reclassified as 'universities', especially since 1992. The intention was to increase the number of 'university graduates' and, quite properly, to attach higher prestige to technical and vocational studies. General academic departments were increased in size or added to these institutions, partly to provide a broadening of studies for technical specialists ('to bridge the gap between the two cultures'); and partly to provide additional full-time degree-level courses for those wishing to study purely non-technical subjects, and so cater for increased numbers of school-leavers who hoped a university qualification would raise their prospects of finding employment at a later date. The exigencies of poor employment prospects thus led to more young people attending general ('academic') courses at new universities, and to a weakening in the specialised link between education and work previously provided by those institutions.[4]

Despite a lower *total* number of university graduates in Switzerland, the numbers graduating in engineering, technological and vocational subjects are much the same there as now in Britain, reckoned per head of the population (as seen in chapter 1). Indeed, it is only following the recent expansion

---

[4] On the danger that 'former polytechnics will seek to become mini-Oxbridges', and that Britain would lose 'its dedicated business-orientated institutions', see the article by C. Price (Principal Emeritus, Leeds Metropolitan University), And then to the university, *Prospect*, October 1995, pp. 88 and 91. The origin of the recent upgrading process goes back at least to the 1966 White Paper which created polytechnics out of those institutions which then had a high proportion of full-time students (studying, for example, for Higher National Diplomas).

of university students in Britain that numbers graduating in engineering reached those of Switzerland, and have begun to approach the German proportion. The example of other countries with higher proportions of university graduates had been held up by international agencies (such as OECD) as a reproach to the Swiss in recent years – even if in truth it should be regarded as largely a nominal matter – and encouraged the Swiss to modify some of their higher technical colleges and reclassify them as technical universities, *Fachhochschulen*. Requirements for mutual international recognition of engineering qualifications (as laid down by the international engineering federation, FEANI) were another factor in this move, together with Swiss employers' hopes for a greater supply of personnel with high vocational skills. In practice, these new *Fachhochschulen* are largely based on an amalgamation of existing higher educational institutions specialising in engineering, commerce, and so on, and provide applied courses at standards corresponding to our applied Bachelor degrees.

Vocational pathways 16–19

Entrance to these technical 'university-level' *Fachhochschulen* is to be expanded on the basis of newly-developed 'vocational A-levels', known as *Berufsmatura*, which correspond to the stated main intentions governing Britain's newly-developed General National Vocational Qualifications at Advanced level. Both cater for 16–19-year-olds, and both can be seen as responses to employers' increased demands for higher-intermediate skills. But the differences between the two countries' development of such qualifications warrant careful attention, particularly as to how they are related to political training and the specificity of careers. In Britain, GNVQs at Advanced level are based mainly on *full*-time courses for *two* years in the sixth-forms of secondary schools or at parallel institutions (Colleges of Further Education, Sixth-form Colleges), and are intended to provide entry to higher education – including general university courses.[5] They cover one of just over a dozen broadly specified vocational areas (business, health and social care, manufacturing, and so on), and are not intended to provide the vocational skills of specific National Vocational Qualifications

---

[5] In practice, 'the preferred progression routes identified by GNVQ students are educational not vocational', and 'very few students expressed an interest in proceeding to an NVQ'; these conclusions were drawn from a survey of 1,100 students by a team led by Professor Alison Woolf: *GNVQs 1993–94* (interim report, Further Education Unit, University of London, and Nuffield Foundation, 1994, pp. 8, 54).

which might be taken subsequently. The scheme is still in its early stages, and it is not clear what proportion of the age group will reach Advanced level – a measure which is often put forward as an indicator of the 'success' of these new qualifications; most young people taking GNVQs will reach only Foundation or Intermediate levels, which are intended to be attainable at age 16+ (discussed further below).

The new Swiss qualifications are based principally on *part*-time courses at a vocational college, extend for *four* years, and accompany a normal apprenticeship. Two days each week are spent at college, of which one day is devoted to general educational subjects and the other to specific vocational subjects; three days a week are spent with an employer providing training under the supervision of a qualified master-craftsman or equivalent. Final examinations are of a dual nature, covering the specific vocational content of a craftsman (as explained in chapter 4) plus written and oral examinations in at least five general educational subjects which are taken to higher standards than for normal apprenticeships. The main differences from the existing Swiss apprenticeships are thus the additional half year or whole year taken by the course overall, and the additional half day or whole day each week to be spent at college. The standard of the courses is such as to be accessible to only about the top tenth of *Sekundarschule* leavers, that is, to about 5 per cent of the total ability range just below those in a *Gymnasium* (say, in the range of the 15–20th percentiles from the top). Entry examinations to the college, usually at age 15+, have to be passed in mathematics (arithmetic, algebra, geometry), German and French. The standard of mathematics required for entry corresponds roughly to GCSE at grade B or, say, Level 8 of the National Curriculum, attained by about the top fifth of pupils in Britain at age 16+; the Swiss examination, as mentioned, is generally taken a year earlier, after completing obligatory schooling at 15+, and the questions are a little more complex.[6]

The *Berufsmatura* to be attained at age nineteen by following this type of course is seen through Swiss eyes as setting a new standard of vocational qualification for young people of this age, and as a development of the

---

[6] The following mathematical examples serve to indicate the standard expected in the Swiss entrance examinations; it should be noticed that, contrary to British practice at GCSE, intermediate steps in the solution are not set out as separate parts of a question, but the specification of optimal steps by the examinee forms an essential component of the task. *Geometry*: A straight cylinder of height 4 cm has a curved surface area of 241.2 cm^2; what is its volume? *Algebra*: Simplify $2y/(x-y) - (x-y)/(x+y) - 4xy/(x^2 - y^2)$.

greatest importance in providing an additional stratum of more highly qualified personnel – additional, that is, to those trained at existing higher educational institutions. To many British eyes it will have a familiar look, in that it mirrors our long-standing arrangements for the training of *technicians*, in contrast to the arrangements for the traditional training of our *craftsmen* (four instead of three years on-the-job training, combined with longer part-time college attendance, higher prerequisite attainments on leaving school, and so on). Swiss *Techniker*, on the other hand, have traditionally received their additional training subsequent to their completion of craft-level courses and after several years of practical experience, say, starting at the age of about 25; those arrangements will continue, though numbers on that route may be depleted by the *Berufsmatura* siphoning off at an earlier age those of higher ability. Inter-country comparisons at this level are clearly complex: for example, the Swiss *Berufsmatura* has a clearly broader subject coverage than the British technician qualification. But what should be of greater interest to the British observer is that the present-day Swiss response to the need for more personnel with high technological skills is to expand the route which combines training at work with additional general education – whereas the main response in Britain has been to broaden full-time educational routes through GNVQs.

A closer parallel to this Swiss development is the new British *Modern Apprenticeship* which was launched in 1995; it was intended to be developed flexibly on an individual basis, and to provide the possibility of subsequent entry to higher education. Acceptance on this scheme requires passes in five subjects in GCSE above grade C (approximately the top half of the attainment range). A 'formal programme of further education' is encouraged *but is not required*; and, contrary to the Swiss approach, there is also no requirement for final external examinations for qualification – whether in general or vocational subjects.[7] The scheme is similar to the traditional apprenticeship in Britain, but is 'modern' – perhaps mainly in not requiring day release for college attendance nor final written examinations! Public subsidies to cover employers' costs of providing training are envisaged via the TEC framework. It is too early to say whether this scheme will attract many young people; about 5 per cent of the age cohort is envisaged (higher proportions are sometimes mentioned; but only very small numbers have been involved in the pilot stage at the time of writing).

[7] Based on the scheme as applied to engineering as described in *The Modern Apprenticeship for Engineering Manufacture* (Engineering Training Authority and Hertfordshire TEC, revd June 1995, p. 6); and *Modern Apprenticeships* (IDS Study 592, December 1995).

Employment orientation during compulsory schooling

The way secondary schooling in Switzerland is more closely oriented to providing school-leavers with a smoother transition to the world of work via an apprenticeship has been outlined in earlier pages. Encouragement to focus on an occupation and career begins at an earlier age and, as explained in chapter 3, the period of work experience while at school at the age of about fourteen is directed, as far as possible, to potential places of apprenticeship. Even if some other career is eventually followed, a pupil of that age who has in mind being accepted for a specific career by a specific employer is stimulated to aim for high standards in the final years of compulsory schooling – certainly in core and vocationally relevant practical subjects, and often in other subjects as well. The experience of excellence is something that Swiss educationists believe should be encouraged for all pupils, even if for some pupils it is possible only in certain practical subjects. The requirement that Swiss *Realschule* teachers are trained in careers guidance undoubtedly helps them encourage pupils in recognising their needs for high attainments in the final phases of their compulsory full-time schooling.

In Britain emphasis continues on 'not foreclosing options at too young an age', and official guidelines to schools continue to insist that the period of work experience should *not* be related to potential employment or potential traineeship, but should form part of only a *general* introduction to the world of work. To be a 'jack of all trades' for as long as possible is considered more important in Britain – even if for a great many school-leavers it may mean that in due course they become 'masters of none'. It must not be forgotten that the advantages of a broad education are by no means neglected in Switzerland, since those proceeding to an apprenticeship continue with general educational subjects on their day-release courses that are part of the requirement for all apprenticeships.

The employment-related incentives provided to Swiss pupils in their final years of compulsory schooling are thus substantially stronger than in Britain, and it is not surprising that lowering of motivation in schooling and truanting at these ages is a complaint much less frequently heard in Switzerland than in Britain. Revision of British official guidelines on work experience seems desirable, though that may first require a reassessment of the fundamental balance of objectives that secondary schools ought to pursue.

Balance of the school curriculum

The need to change the balance of the school curriculum in response to the continuing increase in complexity of work, and decreasing openings for the unskilled, continues to be a matter of concern in both countries. In Britain – to remind ourselves of the main feature of the past decade – there has been the legal specification of a national curriculum for the whole period of compulsory schooling, covering some ten subjects at ages 5–16 (with only slightly reduced requirements at younger ages – for example, no foreign languages in primary schools – and some recent reductions in requirements in the form of 'half subjects'). This type of legislation was a radically new development for central government in Britain (or, more accurately, 'new' since the beginning of this century: before the First World War legislated 'standards' for each year of elementary schooling in core subjects had been officially inspected). The aim of the new National Curriculum was to focus teaching on specified essentials for each subject, reduce unnecessary variability among schools, and raise standards of pupils' attainments. A particular worry to many who were concerned with standards of attainment in core subjects had been the growth of 'cross-curricular' and 'integrated' teaching, especially in primary schools, in which the essentials of school subjects no longer stood out clearly as requiring mastery. The 'process' of learning was given more emphasis than the 'product' or content of learning; the growth of a generalised 'problem-solving' approach in which each pupil was to develop his initiative in thinking around a broad contextualised problem and 'discover' for himself how to tackle it, added to those worries. Average and below-average pupils, with average or below-average teachers, were particularly not well served by these developments. The prime (if usually implicit) ingredient in the remedy provided by the National Curriculum was the refocusing of teaching on specified subjects for which, it might have been thought, there had been a more or less agreed body of content. Of course, externally-set school-leaving examinations had long provided that kind of focus for those pupils in the upper parts of the ability range who had taken O-level examinations (and their predecessors); but the requirements of those examinations had mainly affected the last years of schooling. The new National Curriculum's important features were thus (a) that it applied to all pupils and (b) that it applied throughout the eleven years of compulsory schooling.[8]

---

[8] Special schools, and pupils with special educational needs, were excluded from the requirements.

Experience, however, has increasingly confirmed that fundamental issues remain unresolved in differentiating the curriculum to cater efficiently both for weaker and for stronger pupils. In the rush to effect improvement, many changes – both large issues of principle and smaller points of detail – were inadequately piloted. A principle adopted in Britain from the outset for its National Curriculum is that each subject's components ('Attainment Targets', 'Strands') are to be the same for all pupils, and that individual pupils will differ only in the extent to which they progress through the ten levels that are specified for each component. Thus in mathematics, components are specified (to use familiar terms) for arithmetic, algebra, geometry, probability, data-handling, applications; these are specified from the earliest ages in primary school. The balance among those various components (that is, how much teaching time and degree of mastery) is not however specified; in the absence of official guidance it is presumed by most teachers that each specified component has to be treated equally. Broadly speaking, arithmetic is thus taken to require only about a quarter or a fifth of the teaching time devoted to mathematics as a whole; in actuality, teachers give more emphasis to arithmetic since, as is all too apparent, it is otherwise difficult to make efficient progress in other branches of mathematics.

Educational practice on the Continent, as in Britain in earlier generations, was clear: those pupils not expecting to go on to further or higher education concentrated to a greater extent on mastering arithmetic (including areas and volumes of simple shapes, and basic calculations with rates of interest); algebra and geometry were mainly tackled only by those in more academically-oriented streams of secondary schools. As part of the move to com-prehensive education in Britain in the past generation, and having regard to the need for wider technological competence, such boundary lines within mathematics were deliberately blurred. More difficult topics, and those which require multi-stage analysis by the pupil or long chains of reasoning (such as classical geometrical proofs), were dropped from the syllabuses of even high-attaining pupils; other pupils received instruction in a broader syllabus than previously, though often only the surface of the newer topics was scratched and – more worrying from the point of view of subsequent employment – at a cost in teaching time and mastery of basic arithmetic. Complaints increasingly came from employers and universities that schools were now meeting neither the needs of the 'numerate citizen' nor the needs of those going on to university courses in mathematics, science and engineering.[9]

These complaints have arisen despite the fact that external examinations at the end of the final year of compulsory schooling (GCSE) are set at varying levels of difficulty – usually three 'tiers' in mathematics, two in many other subjects. This differentiation similarly affects the way pupils are set in separate classes according to their attainments. The difficulty, more precisely expressed, is that the blurring in the distinctions among the syllabuses for pupils in different ability groups has led in Britain to a lack of clarity as to which topics are to be *fully mastered* at each level, and which are merely to be *introduced* to varying extents. In Switzerland the distinctions among the mathematics syllabuses for the three or four streams of their secondary schooling system have also tended to narrow in the past generation, partly to encourage higher attainments and partly to facilitate transfer of late-developing pupils; but the syllabuses for individual streams retain their individual character to a greater extent than in Britain, even within the Swiss experimental comprehensive schools. In particular, the Swiss are much clearer on what is appropriate in a mathematics syllabus for those in, say, the lowest tenth or lowest third of the attainment range; and a distinction is drawn in their authorised curriculum for each year and stream of schooling as to whether a new topic is (a) to be introduced, (b) worked through in detail, (c) mastered. [10]

---

[9]   These concerns were evident already at the time of the (official) Cockcroft Committee's report, *Mathematics Counts* (HMSO, London, 1982), and have more recently been voiced with increased urgency by a joint committee (Professor A.G. Howson, chairman) of respected mathematical institutions led by the London Mathematical Society in their report on *Tackling the Mathematics Problem* (1995; on the 'numerate citizen', v. p. 2).

[10]   Based on the *Lehrplan für die Volksschule des Kantons Zürich*, v. esp. p. 259. Changing proportions entering the different secondary streams in Switzerland make difficult any soundly based judgement on trends in attainment of Swiss pupils as a whole. A smaller proportion of all pupils now attends the *Realschule* stream than a decade ago, and a greater proportion attends the *Sekundarschule* stream. Those who have 'upgraded' are likely to be those who in earlier years would have been among the higher attaining pupils in the *Realschule*. Consequently those who now attend the *Realschule* are likely to be of lower average ability than previously and, paradoxical as it may at first seem, the same has to be expected for *Sekundarschulen* – though the average overall for the two streams has not necessarily changed. This 'mathematical paradox' has to be kept in mind when evaluating comments by employers on trends over, say, the past decade. A particular example of a change in the Swiss mathematics curriculum (mentioned to us by employers) was the

More clearly differentiated examinations for secondary schools are still produced by examining boards in Britain. For those for whom modest but practically oriented mathematical attainments are appropriate, these are externally examined Numeracy tests; these tests have been discouraged for most of the past decade by official bodies (including the Schools Curriculum and Assessment Authority), but the tests were not prohibited.[11] At the other end of the spectrum, more academic courses and examinations at that age – continuing the O-level examinations that preceded the current GCSE – and more suited as a basis for subsequent A-level courses taken at 16–18, are still set by English examination boards of the highest repute. They are taken by academically high-achieving pupils in the rest of the world (Singapore, Hong Kong, …) and are marked in England; but they are prohibited to pupils resident in England and Wales.[12]

Despite the varying degrees of commitment by political parties to parental choice in respect of schooling matters, the desire to delay specialisation and provide closely similar syllabuses for all pupils has been decisive so far. While our discussion here has related to the mathematics curriculum – a core subject in everyone's view – much the same has applied to other subjects, including science and practical subjects ('Technology' in the National Curriculum). As seen in chapter 3 above, it is particularly in relation to practical subjects that less-academic pupils are disadvantaged in not being instructed in the exercise of basic skills to high levels – whether it be in

---

removal of basic trigonometry from the *Realschule* curriculum. On the other hand, in comparison with Britain, the Swiss *Realschule* mathematics curriculum still covers many important topics excluded from the lowest tier of GCSE mathematics examinations (which cater for much the same proportion of pupils); for example, area of a circle, application of Pythagoras, volumes of cubes, manipulation of simple linear algebraic expressions with brackets, square roots. The need to keep mathematical instruction at school coherent with the needs of employment and vocational training formed the subject of a Swiss conference held in 1994; see B. Merlo (ed.), *Mathematik an Volksschulen und Berufsbildung* (EDK, 1995, esp. pp. 20–1 on mathematical attainment targets by P. Stoppa).

[11] Numeracy tests and basic literacy tests (Use of English) are set, for example, by the University of London Examinations and Assessment Council (ULEAC), City and Guilds, and the Associated Examining Board.

[12] The University of London and the University of Cambridge boards are examples of boards which continue to set and mark such O-level examinations for pupils in other countries. The basis for their 'illegality' in England and Wales curiously rests on section 5 of the Education Act 1988; but these legal aspects need not detain us here. Exceptionally, the examinations can be taken in England by pupils certified as normally resident abroad.

woodwork, textiles or some other material. High importance is attached by the Swiss to the *direct* benefits in skills and dexterity, and even higher importance to the *indirect* benefits of such instruction – the learning of perseverance, reliability, care, precision, patience. The latter are regarded in Switzerland as the true 'core skills'; in England 'core skills' are now also widely called for, but in practice this refers to little more than the basic literacy and numeracy which a much larger fraction of our school-leavers lack.

As the need became ever clearer in Britain for a more coherent and better focused curriculum for non-academically oriented school-leavers, a move to bring *General* National Vocational Qualifications into the curriculum for 14–16-year-olds was started on a trial basis in 1995; the intention was to provide a better starting point – at so-called Foundation or Intermediate levels – for those hoping to find work at sixteen, and perhaps also for those who might later move to Advanced levels of GNVQ in the sixth form.

Some worries in relation to this initiative can be noted even at the present trial stage. First, like other initiatives originating from the NCVQ stable, lack of clarity in specifying details of the courses to be followed, and lack of attention to reliability in final assessment procedures, must be expected to lower the value and attractiveness of that path. The notion that 'new methods of learning' are to be fundamental in GNVQs is sufficient to raise worries that another generation of youngsters is to be subject to inadequately piloted experimentation. While it is conceivable that fundamental structural reforms may follow the criticisms of NCVQ that are being pressed from all sides while the present lines are being written, there is as yet no real indication that they will go far enough.[13] Secondly, courses in vocational subjects and the associated external examinations in vocational subjects at 16+, which have been taken for many years in secondary schools as part of the GCSE (and its predecessor examinations), are being phased out as part of official policy to encourage GNVQs. No public discussion has taken place on the benefits of eradicating this established and well-understood path to vocational excellence; and it is not clear why the

[13] The officially-sponsored Beaumont *Review of 100 NVQs and SVQs* (pp. 47, n.d., available from Freepost SF10305, Chesterfield) was submitted to the government in January 1996; the GNVQ *Assessment Review* (under Dr Capey; available from NCVQ) was published in November 1995; these reviews followed critical reports by inspectors from Ofsted and FEFC. Further criticism came from a group of fourteen academic researchers in a joint letter to the *Financial Times* (17 January 1996) to the effect that the reforms proposed in the Beaumont report did not go far enough.

principle of consumers' choice (let schools and pupils choose) has been replaced by bureaucratic decision. The lack of clearly stated reasoning why the many decades of experience in this area accumulated by the GCSE examination boards should now be discarded, provides a further indication of the basically unsatisfactory understanding of the realities of school-to-work transition at high bureaucratic levels.

In comparing and assessing the process of transition from school to work in Britain in the context of wider Continental experience, the example of Switzerland examined in this study in practical detail has proved remarkably suggestive and enlightening. Its schooling system has long given great attention to helping the slow-developing or under-achieving child, while at the same time the generality of its pupils reach the highest standards in international tests of schooling attainments. Its vocational training system – though voluntary – is widely accepted as part of the typical school-leaver's maturation and integration into economic life. For the great majority of school-leavers (that is, aside from just over a tenth proceeding to universities) its training system is founded on a younger leaving age from obligatory full-time schooling than in Britain, on high standards in core subjects at school-leaving age, and on a balance of the school curriculum giving greater weight to prerequisites for acceptance as a trainee by employers and vocational colleges. 'Day-release' courses at vocational colleges contain substantial components of continuing general education; the education of young people in Switzerland is thus not regarded as ceasing at age fifteen, when a youngster leaves full-time schooling, but rather as changing its form and locus so as to include – in a systematic and graduated way – increasing elements of workplace and work-oriented instruction. We have also noted the great care taken by the Swiss to ensure that their vocational qualifications have wide marketability and respect, and are based on externally set and externally marked written, oral and practical examinations.

The quantity and quality of output produced by those who have benefited from the Swiss system of education and training have earned the Swiss economy a remarkable position as a producer of advanced high-quality manufactures, and real incomes that are reckoned among the world's highest. In the authors' opinion, the contrasts with Britain in the orientation and implementation of Swiss schooling and training deserve deep consideration by those planning further reforms in Britain.

Appendix A: Statistics of detailed craft-level awards in Britain, Switzerland and Germany, c. 1990

This appendix provides the detailed information underlying table 1.3 of chapter 1 on numbers passing vocational examinations at craft level in five major occupational groups in Britain (1989), Switzerland (1991) and Germany (1991).[1] Names of the occupations in the latter two countries have been translated into English where possible (some specialist occupations do not have an easily understood English counterpart, and have been left in their original language).

Britain[2]

Mechanical engineering
Mechanical engineering craft (205)	1,996
Mechanical engineering maintenance (205)	431
Engineering systems maintenance competences (214)	21
Welding engineering (215)	111
Sheet metal & thin plate (216)	368
Structural & thick plate (217)	174
Mechanical production competence (228)	595
Fabrication and welding competence (229)	272
BTEC National Certificate[3]	5,714
BTEC National Diploma[4]	2,327
TOTAL	12,009

[1] For sources, see footnotes to table 1.3 of chapter 1.
[2] Course reference numbers, where shown in brackets, refer to City and Guilds courses.
[3] Includes BTEC National Certificates in Engineering (Mechanical/Manufacture) and Engineering (Process/Plant/Instrumentation), and an estimated half of BTEC National Certificates in Engineering (remaining half allocated to electrical).
[4] BTEC National Diplomas in Engineering (Mechanical/Manufacture) and an estimated half of BTEC National Diplomas in Engineering (remaining half allocated to electrical).

Electrical engineering

Electrical installation (236)	5,258
Electrical & electronic craft studies (232)	1,258
Electrical servicing (TV, radio, etc.) (224)	1,348
BTEC National Certificate[5]	6,014
BTEC National Diploma[6]	2,431
TOTAL	16,309

Building

Brickwork and masonry (588)	5,972
Carpentry (585–7, 606)	9,015
Plastering, tiling, etc. (590–2, 595/7)	917
Painting and decorating (594)	2,330
Roadwork (614)	200
TOTAL	18,434

Commercial and clerical

BTEC Business and Finance National Certificate	12,162
National Diploma	12,184
RSA/LCCI Private secretary's certificate	1,424
Private and executive secretary's diploma	357
Pitman Institute secretarial group certificate	130
TOTAL	26,257

Retailing

BTEC Distribution Studies National Certificate	160
BTEC Distribution Studies National Diploma	170
Retailing association qualifications and Pitman's Level II[7]	1,000
TOTAL	1,330

[5] BTEC National Certificates in Engineering (Electrical/Electronic) and an estimated half of National Certificates in Engineering.
[6] BTEC National Diplomas in Engineering (Electrical/Electronic) and an estimated half of National Diplomas in Engineering.
[7] Rough estimate (based on discussions with colleges and employers on allocation of total recorded as qualifying at this level).

Switzerland

Mechanical engineering
Mechanical fitter	211
Cutting machinist	10
Precision mechanic	252
Maschinenmechaniker	741
Machinery installation	85
General mechanic	1,145
Machine assembly	422
Smith	68
Toolmaker	262
Jig maker	62
TOTAL	3,258

Electrical engineering
Electronic servicing (audio, video)	156
General electrician	2,760
Electronics	1,018
Electric servicing (TV, radio)	287
Network electrician	101
Switching installations	86
TOTAL	4,408

Building
Floor tiling (including parquet)	224
Roofing	131
Plastering	101
Brickwork	1,074
Painting and decorating	651
Carpentry	2,321
Road work	91
TOTAL	4,593

Commercial

Office clerk	2,579
Commercial clerk	12,656
Commercial diploma (three-year course)	3,220
Commercial diploma (two-year course)[8]	60
TOTAL	19,215

Retailing

Pharmaceutical sundries	341
Pharmaceutical assistant	606
Books	132
Shop assistant[9]	4,460
TOTAL	5,539

Germany[10]

Mechanical engineering

Metal-forming (swarf-producing) (22)	4,125
Solderer (24)	491
Smith (25)	454
Fitter (27)[11]	26,743
Precision mechanic (2840)	3,813
General mechanic (2850)	3,075
Toolmaker (29)	7,245
TOTAL	45,946

[8] Estimate (based on number of students on this course and drop-out rates from three-year course).

[9] About 60 per cent have received specialist training in a specified branch, e.g. sport articles, jewellery, grocery, stationery, furniture, textiles, shoes.

[10] Two-digit numbers refer to occupational groups, four-digit numbers refer to specific occupations within those groups. First-level courses have been excluded to avoid duplication.

[11] Excluding shipbuilder (2752) for comparability with British coverage.

Electrical engineering

Electrical installation (3110)	14,718
Telecommunications (3120)	6,158
Radio, TV (3151)	2,173
Other electricians (31-)[12]	13,978
TOTAL	37,027

Building

Brickwork (44)	5,337
Carpentry (45,50)[13]	15,548
Plastering (48, 4910, 4913)	3,347
Painting (51)[14]	7,538
Road work (46)	1,275
TOTAL	33,045

Office work

Clerical assistant (7810)	5,679
Office clerk (7810)	29,580
Civil servants administrative grade (7811)	11,127
Industrial (7812)	25,965
Legal assistants (7813)	7,712
Other office workers (78-)	1,240
Wholesale and foreign trade (6811)	17,680
Publishing (6831)	849
Transport (7011)	4,476
Travel (7022)	2,376
Marketing (7030)	767
Bank (6910)	20,966
Savings bank (6915)	989
Insurance (6940)	5,296
Full-time qualifications	
- Commercial assistant (781)	3,834
- Foreign language clerk (781)	1,452
- Foreign language secretary (782)	672
- Office work: general (78)	424
TOTAL	141,084

[12] Excluding motor vehicle electricians (3114) for comparability with British coverage.

[13] Excluding occupations 5021–5044 (prototype maker, boat-builder, and so on).

[14] Excluding gilders (5133), decorators of glass, porcelain and ceramics (5140).

Retailing

Retail salesperson (6812, 6813)[15]	25,321
Sales assistant (6820)	10,956
Food (6821)	10,545
Books (6832)	1,361
Music (6833)	69
Pharmaceutical sundries (6841)	536
Pharmaceutical assistant (6851)	3,149
Petrol station attendant (6861)	559
TOTAL	52,496

[15] Excludes half (97 persons) of those qualified as *Einzelhandelskaufmann* (6812) assumed to have previously obtained a qualification as sales assistant (6820).

Appendix B: Vocational qualifications awarded in Britain after the establishment of NCVQ

The establishment of the National Council for Vocational Qualifications in Britain in 1986 was intended to increase the number of persons attaining qualifications within a new all-embracing and coherent framework. It was difficult to judge the success of this initiative in its early years because 'time inevitably needed to elapse to overcome teething problems'. Now that nine years have passed it is not unreasonable to look at the available figures of the number of persons attaining the new-style qualifications: indeed, to delay longer in assessing developments runs the risk of allowing the situation to deteriorate further, with increased difficulties of counter reforms. We disregard in this Appendix the serious reservations attached to the reliability of the new methods of assessing candidates for qualification (discussed in chapter 4), and present simply the total number of NVQ awards at Level 3 – ostensibly equivalent to the 'craft level' previously widely recognised in this country (equivalent to City and Guilds part II, and so on).

Putting together awards in the five main occupational groups that we compared internationally in chapter 1, we arrive at a total of 9,000 NVQs awarded in 1994 (see table B.1). This is equivalent to a total of a mere 1.3 per cent of all 19-year-olds in the country; it compares with a total of 9.2 per cent who received awards in these five occupational groups in 1989 under pre-NCVQ schemes in Britain, and with 42 per cent who received awards at corresponding levels in those five occupational groups in Switzerland and Germany (chapter 1, table 1.3).

The awards counted here for 1994 relate to unexpired NVQs which are published by detailed subject title and Level in the *NVQ Monitor*; they exclude totals of expired NVQs published in the *Monitor* but not classified by detailed subject title nor Level. If we are to include an estimate of awards for expired qualifications it might increase the 1.3 per cent just mentioned to 1.7 per cent; and an allowance for other awarding bodies not covered here might raise the total to some 2 per cent. But such adjustments hardly alter the substance of the comparison.[1] Insofar as NCVQ may claim greater success, it may well be at Level 2; this corresponds only (and probably not quite) to the intermediate level of qualification on the Continent and to our previous City and Guilds part I. Such awards are usually gained at the end of the first year of apprenticeship, whereas craft-level awards are gained after usually three years; the former category is of no real concern in comparison with Continental skill levels.

The true decline in training and skills in the country since NCVQ came on the scene may not be as great as these figures suggest because some courses and qualifications have continued under previous schemes organised by City and Guilds (and similar organisations) requiring rigorous external and written tests; and also because some employers have opted for internal training arrangements – even if it meant sacrificing government training subsidies – to avoid heavy NCVQ bureaucratic formalities. Such 'internal qualifications' may well be of benefit within large firms, but they lack the reliability and marketability that would benefit a well-functioning market for skills.

Following NCVQ-inspired reforms, many qualifications are now awarded on a modular or unitised basis, each of which is returned separately in the statistics of awards. There is now no way for an external observer to combine published statistical returns on awards of *modules* by City and Guilds (and by other examining bodies of that kind) with NVQ statistical returns in order to reach a total for the country as a whole of the number of *persons* each year reaching craft-level qualifications, in such a way as to avoid multiple counting. The *Statistical Bulletin* on *Awards of Vocational Qualifications* (issued by the Department for Education and Employment in December 1995) refers to a total of 1,010, 000 vocational awards in 1993/94 at all levels; there are only some 700,000 persons per age cohort, and much double counting of the number of persons involved has clearly taken place (at the time of writing we understand that further elucidation is planned by government statisticians).[2]

[1] All that we are given in the *Monitor* on expired NVQs are the total awards for *all* Levels together for ten broad occupational groups; these expired awards in 1994 amounted to a third of the unexpired awards in the four occupational groups most relevant to our present comparisons: construction, engineering, manufacturing, providing goods and services (groups 3,4, 5 and 7).

[2] An attempt by the Department of Employment to establish a new National Information System for Vocational Qualifications has so far yielded only meagre results. These are broadly consistent for NVQs with those in table B.1 for a narrower set of occupations. It is clear that even within official circles there are now immense difficulties in combining, for any *individual* trainee, the components ('modules',

Table B.1 *NVQ Level 3 awards in 1994 in five occupational groups*

	No. of awards	% of all 19 year-olds[a]
Mechanical[b]	770	0.1
Electrical	-	-
Construction	2,153	0.3
Office work[c]	5,571	0.8
Retailing[d]	371	0.05
Total	8,865	1.3

Source: *NVQ Monitor*, Winter 1994/95 (cumulative totals to 4 November 1994, less corresponding cumulative totals till September 1993: approx. 13 months).

Notes:

[a]Taking the number of 19-year-olds as 680,000 in England and Wales.

[b]Includes NVQs in engineering and manufacturing (excludes vehicle maintenance).

[c]Includes GNVQ administration

[d]Includes on-licensed premises supervisory management, customer service, selling residential property.

In short, there is no evidence so far that NCVQ has led to any increase in the annual number of persons attaining recognised craft qualifications; on the contrary, it seems more likely that there has been a serious decline – to the unfortunate detriment of this country's young people and its economy. Unfortunately also, no adequate provision was made within the machinery of government for the compilation of relevant national totals; the means of knowing where the country now stands, in relation to earlier years or other countries, still needs to be established.

'units') he may have been recorded as passing in order to arrive at the total number of persons who have attained a *full* qualification (see B. Sheppard and P. Smalley, NISVQ – a new database on vocational education and training, *Employment Gazette*, June 1993, esp. pp. 291 and table 1).

Appendix C: Socialisation of pupils in Swiss schooling

Swiss schoolteachers place much emphasis on the socialisation of pupils in their classroom (termed *Menschenbildung*, see chapter 2, p. 28) both as a precondition for efficient learning and as a valued objective in itself. This approach is illustrated in the following three notes, (1) from a Swiss official report on primary schooling, (2) by a Swiss secondary school teacher, and (3) an incident illustrating 'democratic' self-imposed social discipline observed in a Swiss class by our team. To some extent these notes illustrate ideals rather than average practice: nevertheless, the contrast with Britain is undoubtedly real and – in the view of our visiting teams of English teachers and school inspectors – deserves deep consideration.

(1) Social integration in primary schooling (from an official report)

An extended official inquiry into possible improvements in primary schooling in the Canton of Zürich began in 1975 and led to a final report in 1992.[1] It included a section on communication as a 'socially integrating' process, and on the importance of 'talking to one another'. The following is a free translation.

How can relations between teachers and pupils be made cooperative instead of confrontational? We propose three principles of good practice:-

[1] *Überprüfung der Primarschule im Kanton Zürich: Schlussbericht SIPRI* (Erziehungs-direktion Zürich, 1992), p. 51. The short section translated here from that report had been abstracted from a more detailed report on 'breaking down barriers in the course of teaching' prepared for that inquiry: *Belastungsabbau im Unterricht* by N. Landwehr with O. Fries, P. Hubler and the SIPRI-Schools at Bäretswil and Bülach, ED, Zürich, 1984, pp. 16–29.

A participative approach to education The teacher should treat her pupils with respect and understanding. She should endeavour to approach them in the same way as she expects them to approach her. She should aim to keep direct orders to a minimum.

Democratic resolution of disputes Disputes should be resolved, not by authoritarian means, but with the help of discussion aimed at recognising and eliminating conflicts of interests, listing possible solutions, and evaluating them. Which solution might be acceptable to all involved? How can it be put into practice? The consequences of the accepted solution should subsequently be assessed in the light of experience.

Communication as a teaching theme Children need to learn – and need to be taught – how to communicate without embarrassment (or shyness); the teacher can help by encouraging discussion during lessons and through role-play.

(2) The teacher as social pedagogue (by Frau T. Sprock, Zürich)[2]

The extract below is from a recent article on the teacher as Educator *(conceptually distinct in Continental terms from* Instructor*); it describes the first days at the beginning of the school year when pupils enter their new* Sekundarschule *and the teacher carefully lays foundations for a cooperative learning environment. The pupils come from a variety of primary schools; they are mostly aged twelve, and most will stay with the same teacher for the next three years. As explained in chapter 2, the form teacher in this category of secondary school teaches these pupils nearly half of all school subjects, and most of the other half are taught by the form teacher of the parallel class. The distinct conversational style ('register', as the linguists say) of the Swiss teacher has been preserved as far as possible in this translation; it is closer to that of a reassuring but demanding parent guiding his or her children, rather than – as often among English teachers – to*

---

[2] Frau Sprock has taught at Swiss primary schools and at various types of Swiss secondary schools, including a comprehensive secondary school. For reasons of space, this appendix presents only just over a half of the original article; the original was based on a talk entitled *Der Lehrer als Erzieher: Lehrer-Schüler-Beziehung und Klassenunterricht* (published in *Menschenkenntnis*, Zürich, 10/92, pp. 30–44). The translation is by Fiona Thirlwell (NIESR).

a sergeant struggling to maintain his platoon's progress.[3] *The English reader will notice the emphasis given in this Swiss account to whole-class teaching (that is, not teaching separate groups within a classroom), and to the avoidance of any form of mocking behaviour.*

The teacher supports and consolidates the important socialisation task which has begun in the parents' home, much in the way that the mother in the first years of a child's life develops a social relationship with her child and helps him gradually widen his social contacts both within the family and outside it. It is possible for the teacher also to compensate to some extent for shortcomings and inadequacies of earlier childhood. The teacher tries to understand each child and to support his individual personality. He seizes on and encourages positive attitudes in the child, helps in overcoming weaknesses, and at the same time counteracts any tendencies towards unsocial behaviour. Many difficult behavioural problems in children can be overcome once it is possible to involve the child in a friendly class community; and a child who feels appreciated and who has been successful in his learning ceases to be disruptive. A developed sense of social interest is closely connected with the development of intellectual abilities. A cooperative pupil shows consideration for others, likes to help his neighbour, gains friends, feels more secure, is more attentive, hears more and sees more, is interested in his surroundings, his memory absorbs more – and all this contributes to increased achievement in learning. Whole-class teaching is especially suited to create such a sense of community.

On the first day of school for new pupils at my *Sekundarschule* a great variety of faces look at me expectantly: some are anxious, some are well-behaved; others are nervous, restrained or reserved and observe the proceedings with mistrust; they may be sitting next to pupils who are loud, cheeky, domineering or who get up to nonsense. Some are already able to learn well, others have less success. In their new secondary school the

---

[3] An excellent survey-based account of English teachers' first days in their new class noted that *experienced* teachers were the first to establish 'varying degrees of dominance by restricting pupils' movements ... [pupils] only come out when I tell them to. You [the teacher] give the directions.' Begin a lesson 'with some from of criticism like, "you don't call this lined up, do you? LINE UP!"'. When two boys were chatting, the teacher 'barked out in a very loud and frightening voice, "Did I ask you to talk?" He paused for two seconds in the ensuing silence and stared. "Well, don't then"' (from E.C. Wragg and E.K. Wood, Teachers' first encounters with their classes, ch. 3 in E.C. Wragg (ed.), *Classroom Teaching Skills*, Croom Helm, 1984, pp. 54, 65, 69).

latter often sit in their seats – but not participating, behaving coldly towards all and especially towards adults, and follow the teaching only reluctantly.

Children from different social and national backgrounds sit in front of me. Each has developed his individual way of behaving in a group and at school. Nevertheless, they all have much in common. Apart from being of much the same age and development, they have completed the same years of primary school. It is certain that they all want to be accepted by their teacher and by their fellow pupils, and hope to get on well with their colleagues and to make 'at least' one close friend. They are apprehensive of their new situation and concerned whether they will be able to meet the demands made of them. On these common characteristics of human nature I build my work and discussions with the whole class.

A new class always seems to me like a mirror image of society. If a teacher succeeds in forming a real community – in which everyone is accepted, no one is excluded, and everyone is aware that their contribution has an important effect on the community as a whole – then each pupil feels secure and can learn in a more relaxed manner. Pupils' confidence in their classmates, in their teachers and in themselves improves as a result of their experience of being together in a good class community, and it strengthens them. They take that confidence with them into their subsequent classes and later on into their office or place of work. This experience of feeling that they are living together gives them confidence in their fellow human beings and influences their future friendships and relationships.

A class community that has developed to the level just described does not simply happen on its own: it requires intensive careful nurturing and a conscious structuring of pupils' school lives by the teacher. The teacher focuses on his pupils: he guides them and encourages them. When they are successful, he praises them; when unsuccessful, he urges them to try again. All his efforts are geared to helping each pupil to succeed and so strengthen his individuality. Success means that the pupil can make progress in relationships with his friends and in his learning.

When we became acquainted with one another on the first day that these pupils attended their new school, I told the pupils what I have found important for successful cooperation. 'Some of you', I said, 'already know one another from former classes, but most do not. It will take a little time for us to get to know everyone, and it is important that as soon as possible we all feel happy together in this new class. It is up to us how we treat one another. If we are all considerate to one another and everyone is accepted, then you will all the more enjoy coming to school and will be able to learn better. I will show you how you can work so that you are successful, and also how you can become friends. I will tell you when you do something well, and I will also let you know if I am not pleased with something. We will then discuss exactly how you can do better. I want you to do the same: if you have not understood something, or do not agree with a situation, come and speak to me about it. In this way we will learn to trust one another.' The pupils listened attentively and some showed their agreement by nodding. I continued: 'In order that we get to know each other's names quickly, write your name on a card and put it in front of you. Your first homework for the end of the week will be to learn all the names and to have at least one short conversation with each pupil in the class. On Friday you will talk about it in the language lesson (German).' The pupils thought these tasks fun, and noted them in their homework diaries.

At this first meeting with the new class some small details betrayed sensitivities and fears; these indicated to me what I had to watch out for with this or that pupil. For example, when the name-card of one pupil was missing that afternoon, I asked him to put it back. He beamed at me and said, 'I am René.' I told him that I needed two to three days to get to know the names of both the parallel classes thoroughly. He nodded in understanding and said, 'You know mine now'; nevertheless he put his card back.

I did not pay too much attention to the incident, but after the break his name-card had again disappeared. Immediately I asked him, 'René, where is your card?' He smiled and said, 'You don't need it any more, you know me.' 'Yes, you are right,' I said, 'I know you now.' In a charming way he had managed to make sure that his was one of the first names I learnt, and my statement had reassured him for the moment. My inference that he greatly feared that he might not be accepted by me and his classmates was soon confirmed. He was so nervous that not only his hands shook, but his whole body vibrated. Several months of careful work were necessary before René felt sufficiently secure to learn with more peace of mind. I only learnt his history later from his mother, which brought further understanding of his feelings.

The next day I again looked at the faces in front of me. I had already established an initial rapport with two pupils who seemed insecure; but there was also Christoph – who did not look up, and whom I had not yet seen speaking to anyone. Then there was Sabine, who looked at me with mistrust, and when I looked at her she looked down again quickly. And over there sat Roland, the biggest in the class. He lay back on his chair sleepily, making his uneasiness with school evident. And right at the front there was Daniel, chattering: he was usually the first to put his hand up, and was dreadfully angry when another pupil was allowed to answer. I resolved to speak to these pupils individually as soon as possible.

Roland had been immediately noticeable on the first morning; he strolled into the classroom and remained standing hesitantly next to the other pupils. He greeted me, but without looking at me; eye-contact was impossible. He was one of the maturest pupils, his voice had already broken, and he stood out through his emphasised casual attitude. He groaned at the smallest challenge – for example, when discussing the timetable – and made it clear that it was all too much for him. On the first meeting of the class he told us that he had been at a private school for three years because he had not got on well with his teachers at the state primary school. Some pupils remembered him from the fourth class [of the state primary school]. When I asked him if he wanted to stay here, he answered, 'If I like it.' 'Do you not like work? Surely you were made to work hard at the private school.' 'It was OK,' was his reply, accompanied by a shrug. I noticed how especially the younger-looking pupils looked at him admiringly; his careless manner impressed them. In the next few days he regularly arrived late, often left his things at home or had not completed his work. During lessons he obviously picked things up quickly; he was generally very quiet, but often whispered a comment to his neighbour after I had spoken. He tried to stir up opinion against the school and the teachers. I knew little about his life history, but I encouraged him to have more to do with the others. I invited him to join in, and I gave him to understand that I expected more from him. He started to adapt, but he seemed to feel constantly pressurised; his achievements seemed significantly below his capability.

A conversation at a parents' evening made things clearer. His father had studied at university, and the elder son had evidently inherited his father's intelligence and was at a *Gymnasium* (grammar school). The parents thought from an early age that Roland should go in a different direction. That was very difficult for him, but the parents thought they ought not to push him to achieve more than he was capable of. His teachers had come to a different conclusion about his capabilities, but we all knew at the same time that only Roland could convince his parents of his latent talents. Some days later I spoke to the pupils individually about their attainments. I told Roland that my discussions with his teachers confirmed that he was a very bright pupil; he had a good ability to grasp new things, but he still had some gaps from his primary school. If he would really start studying, it would be easy for him to become one of the best pupils and go on to a *Gymnasium* later. A disparaging hand movement, and 'That doesn't interest me anyway', were his only visible reactions. Nevertheless, within a few days Roland was working more carefully and seemed more interested in the world. Much further encouragement was necessary, so that he would avoid failure and build up the necessary patience to continue even when success was not immediately forthcoming. It was a long time before he felt able to tell me that he quite liked studying after all. The jump that he made when he first got a top mark in a test was sufficient evidence for my deduction that it was the competitive situation at home with his sibling that had made school unpleasant for him. His fellow pupils followed Roland's efforts with interest, and we were all pleased for him on his progress. He served as an example to others, and had proved that progress can be made through more study. When after his very good test result he got a significantly lower mark in the next test he came to me and asked if he could discuss what had gone wrong. That was the beginning of real cooperation.

However, let us return to the Friday of the first week when the pupils talked about their 'getting to know one another' conversations: they had taken the task I had set them very seriously, and one after another reported to the class. When the first eight pupils had all mentioned Christoph as among those not spoken to, I interrupted and asked Christoph whom he had spoken to. He answered, 'With my neighbours on the left and right.' 'Is that all? Why not the others?' He shrugged his shoulders and stared at the bench in front of him. I then asked the pupils: 'Why did you not speak to him? Then he would have spoken to many of you; I don't understand.' At first everyone was hesitant; then one pupil said she was afraid of Christoph because he always looked so gloomy. She also thought that he didn't like it when she wanted to speak to him. I answered, 'You don't have to be afraid of Christoph, I have already spoken to him a few times, he really is a nice person. Perhaps he can tell us later why he has been so quiet until today. I am sure he would be very pleased if you spoke to him; why don't you try to do so by next Friday?' When I said he would be very pleased, Christoph glanced up thankfully at me. The pupils agreed immediately, and a week later said that they had enjoyed speaking to him and had done so several times. Some reported that he had approached them and begun a conversation.

For a long time Christoph found it difficult to mix with the class; but his classmates were inventive and persistent. In the meantime it had become apparent that he tended to stop in the middle of test papers, as soon as first doubts arose. When I once looked up on such an occasion, I heard his neighbour say loudly, 'Don't you dare give up, just keep writing!' His neighbour winked at me, and we both noticed with pleasure how Christoph began to work again. I could write a book about this growing cooperation between Christoph and the whole class; I have to emphasise that without the active help of the pupils it would not have been possible to give this boy the strength to begin to feel valued in the class, to make mistakes and learn along with the others. His fellow pupils learnt how to develop their human sympathies, and were strengthened by understanding how important their help had been.

It is necessary for pupils to treat each other pleasantly if real friendships are to develop. In the first days and weeks we discussed this topic on many occasions. If a pupil made a mistake in the lesson and the others laughed, or threw each other knowing glances, I explained to them that there is never a reason to make fun of another person. 'It is a very delicate matter, and there is a risk that in a few weeks nobody responds in class unless they are entirely sure of the answer. If that became the case, we could no longer study together as effectively. It would be better in such a situation if you all tried to find out what the other has not understood, and then try and explain it to him.' Most pupils were initially not aware that their mocking reactions had an inhibiting effect on others, but some told the class how uncomfortable they felt when others laughed; their mistake then felt twice as bad. After that the class resolved to give up this habit. The pupils were proud of themselves – and that was the best move towards further learning.

Most pupils quickly decide not to mock each other in class; outside the class – in the break, on the way home or when the teacher is absent – it becomes more difficult to give up ingrained behaviour such as continual 'leg-pulling'. Pupils say to me, 'It is only a bit of fun, don't you see young people like having fun?' 'I understand you very well,' I said, 'but to this day I still have not met any pupil who is pleased when a colleague puts a leg out and trips him up. Or like yesterday, when one of you took your best friend's fountain pen, hid it in the waste-paper basket and left him alone in the classroom after the lesson to look for it. Is that supposed to be fun? Did you find it funny Andreas?' 'No,' he answered, 'it was fun only for the others.' 'Then tell me what is funny if a girl trips over an out-stretched leg onto the hard stone floor. And you laugh. What do you think would be a proper reaction?' 'Someone could help her up,' suggested one pupil. 'That would be behaviour better befitting young people, like yourselves,' I said, 'and you could then consider how to speak to your friend who had tripped her.' Some continued to try and convince me of the harmlessness of their fun, but gradually more pupils began to support me and tried to change the way they behaved to each other.

I held many such simple conversations with the class during lessons, at break-time and after school. I would like to explain why they were significant. A real change in pupils' behaviour is possible only if they have decided to do it themselves. They then accept it, and are pleased if they succeed. As a teacher I consider it my duty to strengthen the wish in every pupil to be pleasant to others, and to learn better. Arguments and conflicts are discussed openly in the classroom wherever possible, so that all pupils can experience together that it is not about finding the guilty and the innocent, but always about how 'opposite sides' in a conflict can make peace again, and how differences can be resolved peacefully. A class which begins to talk and laugh together, instead of *at* one another, begins at the same time to learn together. Comparisons with fellow pupils and healthy competition are effective incentives in whole-class learning. Pupils learn to express their individual desires, while at the same time taking into consideration the needs of others.

On this basis it is possible to teach pupils to help one another both at school and at home. For example, one pupil is happy about his marks in language (German), but at the same time he also sees his neighbour is upset at his own unsatisfactory marks. He wonders how he might help him; he invites him to study together on a free afternoon, or they both come to me and we consider together what support would be best. Many of my pupils study together in groups of two or three, especially before tests.

Another example: I was once late in getting to class after attending a meeting. I was used to the fact that the pupils had already learnt to talk to one another and, when I am late, study something by themselves or test each other. On that occasion I was nevertheless astonished on my return to observe quietly at the door that Reto was sitting on my chair and was practising vocabulary with the class. He was so engrossed that he noticed me only when the pupils began to smile. He turned to me and said, 'I'll give you your seat back; but can I first finish this row of words?' I nodded and watched him happily. When Reto offered me my chair, I nodded to him and to the whole class in acknowledgement, and I said, 'This is how I imagine the school of the future: pupils of their own accord use their time to learn together.'

How does the teacher create such a learning atmosphere? He does not just sit back and let his pupils express themselves: rather, he takes great pains to develop a close understanding of each pupil individually. He develops a wide knowledge of human behaviour and empathy. It is of course also important that he is aware of his own subconscious feelings so that no distortions disturb his relationships with pupils. A greater ability to relate to people enables him to teach his pupils with understanding.

(3) Self-imposed classroom discipline

Observed by our visiting team. The precise incident requiring discipline is probably more widely tolerated in Swiss schools than this account may suggest; however, the process of joint agreement on acceptable rules of behaviour while in class can be considered as representative of wider Swiss ideals (of course, not wholly unknown in England, but certainly not typical).[4]

On one of our first visits to a Swiss secondary school (a *Realschule*, for non-academic pupils) our team of four observers sat at the back of a class of about twenty boys and girls aged 13–14 and watched a lesson in mathematics. The lesson proceeded in an orderly way and was in its main oral-participative phase (as described in chapter 2), with a succession of graded questions and probes from the teacher, and answers by pupils from their desks or spoken at the front of the room and written by them on the wall-board or OHP transparency. In the middle of this phase, without any other very noticeable disturbance, one of the girls stood up, walked to one of the back corners of the room and stood there facing the wall; the only possible associated event that we noticed at the time had been a barely audible couple of words from the teacher in her general direction. The remainder of the class continued as if nothing had happened. After about a quarter of an hour facing the wall, the girl and the teacher looked at their watches, and the girl returned to her desk and continued working normally.

At the end of the lesson our team held a brief discussion with the teacher on many general aspects of the lesson; finally, we mentioned the curious behaviour of this individual pupil. It was a long story, he explained. At the beginning of the previous school year, when these pupils transferred from primary to secondary school and first joined his class, he had organised a series of discussions on appropriate rules of behaviour to enable the whole class to learn efficiently; these formed part of the native-language lessons, intended to promote precise oral expression and at the same time develop pupils' social concerns. Among the matters discussed was eating in class, including the appropriateness of chewing gum in class. Each aspect was discussed *pro* and *con*, with the teacher raising relevant considerations as

---

[4]   These ideals can be traced in the writings of the Swiss educationist J. Piaget (published in England in 1932, *The Moral Judgement of the Child*, Routledge, p. 365f.), where he objects to the views of the noted French sociologist Durkheim, and commends the 'democratic' school system of the Englishman(!) Sanderson, as described by H.G. Wells (*The Story of a Great Schoolmaster: Being a Plain Account of the Life and Ideas of Sanderson of Oundle*, London, Chatto & Windus, 1924; it will not be overlooked that Oundle was a well-resourced private school catering for the children of the wealthier classes). No doubt these ideas and debates have a long history; it is of interest that the current Japanese approach is similar to Piaget's, as noted by J. Hendry (Kindergarten and the transition from home to school education, *Comparative Education*, 1986, p. 57).

necessary. Eating was decisively determined by the class to be inappropriate; on gum-chewing, the discussion was less decisive and had to be continued as part of the following day's lesson. At the end, the class rejected it. On the third day the teacher suggested that it would be right to debate whether sanctions – verbal reproofs or some form of punishment – should apply to those who offended against the class's agreed code; and, if so, what sanction would be proportionate to each type of misdemeanour. The class decided that fifteen minutes facing the wall in a classroom corner was appropriate for gum-chewing. He therefore had simply to say to that pupil, 'Gum-chewing?'– and that was sufficient for her to go to the corner without further ado.

There is no need to elaborate here on the many admirable aspects of Swiss socio-political life reflected in this incident, and on the role of the school-teacher in the transmission and propagation of the widely accepted consensus on democratic social processes. The agreed punishment in this class may seem old-fashioned and unusual; but such ways of agreeing on classroom rules of behaviour are widely accepted in Swiss schools (so we were informed). There is clearly a considerable gap between their approach to the socialising role of a school and what can be considered as realistically imaginable in the corresponding English context.

Appendix D: A Swiss experiment in comprehensive schooling

As in other countries, there have been pressures in Switzerland to establish comprehensive secondary schools catering for a broad range of abilities within the same building. But the Swiss have moved slowly and cautiously. In the Canton of Zürich just over a dozen schools in a few school districts have moved experimentally to a comprehensive form since the end of the 1970s; they now (1994) account for about a tenth of all secondary pupils in the Canton. During the 1980s the mathematical attainments of pupils in these experimental schools were compared with a matched sample of schools in comparable districts which followed the traditional selective pattern. The results of these comparisons are of wider interest and are summarised here for the benefit of English readers; the discussion has been taken a little further than in the original Swiss report, with somewhat different implications.[1]

The comparisons were based on a total of 800 secondary pupils, consisting of two age cohorts who had finished primary schooling in the summers of 1984 and 1985 respectively; the pupils were tested at the end

[1] The account given here is based on the original report by S. Rosenberg, *Leistungsuntersuchung in Mathematik: Vergleich zwischen AVO und dreigliedriger Oberstufe während den Schuljahren 1983/84 bis 1986/87* (Pestalozzianum Zürich, report no. 27, duplicated, 1987); we are grateful to Frau Rosenberg and her colleagues for discussing the issues with us. Similar and even more detailed comparisons were carried out for comprehensive and selective schools in certain German *Länder* at about that time, for example, by K. Aurin, B. Schwarz and R.-D. Thiel, *Gegliedertes Schulsystem und Gesamtschule: Vergleichsuntersuchung des Landes Baden-Württemberg* (Ministerium für Kultur und Sport, Stuttgart, 1986, v. esp. the concluding chapter by Professor Aurin, vol. II, p. 346), and several articles in the *Zeitschrift für Pädagogik*, October 1980, on Nordrhein-Westfalen and Austria. We are not aware of any similar comparisons for Britain before the widespread adoption of comprehensive schooling.

of their primary school (at about age twelve), and then again after two years in their various secondary schools (at about age fourteen).

The traditional selective secondary schooling system in Zürich – as explained in chapter 2 – consists of four levels of schooling which we may here call simply A, B, C and D. The top level A (the *Gymnasium*, accounting for just over a tenth of all pupils) was retained as a separate type of school; it was only the lower three levels B, C and D – accounting for nearly nine tenths of all pupils – which were combined into a new 'experimental' comprehensive type of school which became known as AVO.[2] Each AVO school was divided into two ability *streams* for almost all subjects; the exceptions were mathematics and the first foreign language – French – for which pupils were divided into three *sets* (*Niveaugruppen*) on the basis of their attainments in each subject. For mathematics there is therefore a degree of correspondence between the old B, C and D selective schools and the three sets in the new AVO comprehensive school. It was the attainments of pupils in these three paired levels that formed the basis of the Swiss comparisons. Different mathematics syllabuses and textbooks applied to each of the three levels in both the old and new systems: but much the same syllabuses were used at corresponding levels in the two systems. Mathematics tests were accordingly designed by teachers for each of the three levels, and administered to pupils in both systems.

The results are summarised in table D.1. They show no difference in attainments at level C (the *Realschule*), where pupils in both the old and new types of school obtained an average score of 53 per cent (see right-hand side of table). But at the higher and lower levels (B and D) pupils in comprehensive schools did not do as well as in the traditional selective schools.

Low-attaining pupils

These differences need to be discussed in more detail, taking into account the individual organisational features of some of the sample schools. Let us begin with the lowest level of attainment, where pupils of the traditional selective system (*Oberschulen*) obtained an average score of 34 per cent while pupils in the comparable level of the comprehensive system on the same test averaged a score of only 27 per cent. This probably does not express the full extent of the gap between the systems, since the set of low-attaining pupils in the comprehensive system accounted for 16 per cent

---

2   Short for *Abteilungsübergreifende Versuche an der Oberstufe* (roughly: over-arching multi-lateral experiment at the secondary level).

of all pupils, compared with only 9 per cent of pupils in the selective system (see left-hand side of table D.1). Because of its greater breadth, the comprehensive low set should be expected to include pupils who are higher in their average *general* ability than were included in the selective stream; there is a possible offsetting factor in that, in terms of *mathematical* ability, the comprehensive schools might have been more effective in selecting pupils who were weak in that subject alone, rather than in all subjects taken together (the criterion for pupils in the selective system). However, this offset is unlikely to be large since mathematical and general attainments – while not identical – have a fairly strong positive correlation. On the whole therefore, we should still expect the wider band of comprehensive pupils would have done better, and not worse, than the corresponding selective pupils.

If we were to base our comparisons – as we should – on the *same proportion* of pupils in both systems, we would need to know the average score of the lowest 9 per cent of pupils in the comprehensive system (out of the 16 per cent actually in that set). That might reduce the average score for comprehensive pupils from the recorded 27 per cent to under 20 per cent.[3] The true gap between the systems at this lower end of the attainment range is thus between a score of 34 per cent for selective schools and an approximate score of under 20 per cent for the comprehensive schools.

The estimated gap between the systems would be reduced if we omit an unusual low-attaining class in one of the comprehensive schools (school G, class e2). This school integrated Special pupils (*Sonderklässler*) in one of the two years of these comparisons; the lowest mathematical set was described as having included some ('*einige*') of these pupils, leading to an average score for that class of a mere 3 per cent.[4] The class consisted of seven pupils; though only *some* were Special pupils, it seems that other pupils in that class also had made very little progress. Omitting that class in its entirety from the comparisons would raise the average score in that lowest comprehensive stream from the recorded 27 per cent to 30 per cent;

[3] The true average score for the lowest 9 per cent could have been obtained from the original records (but they are no longer available). For the present purposes we made estimates of the original frequency distributions based on the published information for each school of the minimum and maximum scores, together with averages and standard deviations (Rosenberg, table 31). Removing the top slice (between the 9th and 16th percentiles) left an average score of only 14 for the lowest 9 per cent of pupils; to allow for imperfect correlation between general and mathematical attainments we have roughly raised the estimate average score to 'under 20 per cent' in the text above.

[4] See pp. 9 and 23–4 of the original report.

Table D.1 *Mathematical attainments of samples of 14-year-old pupils in comprehensive and selective schools, Switzerland 1986 and 1987*

	Percentage of pupils		Average scores at age 14[a]	
Set/level[b]	Comprehensive sample	Selective sample	Comprehensive sample	Selective sample
B Sekundarschule	53[c]	55	56[c]	63
C Realschule	31	36	53	53
D Oberschule	16	9	27[d]	34
	100	100		

Source: Rosenberg, *op. cit.* (see fn. 1).
Notes:
[a]The original test scores were based on a varying numbers of questions and points (set/level A: 24; B: 22; C: 19); they have here all been converted into percentages.
[b]Name of level in selective system; different tests were applied to each level.
[c]One of the larger comprehensive schools (P) was divided into four ability levels; the second level 'BC' can be considered as roughly equivalent to the lower part of what, in other schools, formed level B. On that basis, level B (excluding BC) accounted for 38 per cent of all pupils in the comprehensive sample, and attained an average score of 64 per cent; and level BC accounted for 15 per cent of all pupils in the comprehensive sample, and attained an average score of only 35 per cent (all measured on the same test; see text).
[d]If school G is excluded, the average rises to 30 per cent (see text).

the estimated score for the lowest 9 per cent of comprehensive pupils – for comparison with the corresponding percentage in the selective schools – might rise from the less than 20 per cent suggested above to, say, under 23 per cent. That still leaves a substantial contrast with the score of 34 per cent recorded for the average selective school at that level (the *Oberschule*).

As emphasised in the original report by Rosenberg, the two samples of schools were matched in terms of parental occupation, national origin and language. Parents in both types of Swiss school districts were not offered a *choice* between comprehensive and selective schools (as usual in those parts of Germany where comprehensive schools are available): pupils were directed to a local school on the basis of official policy in each district. There should therefore be no reason to suspect that, as a result of 'creaming', pupils of lower calibre went to comprehensive as compared with selective schools.[5] It therefore seems that there was a relative deterioration among low-achieving pupils who happened to be living in districts where they were required to attend comprehensive secondary schools.

It is always possible that the test given to pupils at this level was not well-designed to display the true attainments of such pupils, or that there were changes in teaching materials or teaching styles which needed more time to settle down effectively.[6] A repeat of such comparisons thus seems desirable, especially since several more years have now elapsed during which the new system has been able to settle down.

High-attaining pupils

For the upper set an analogous contrast was observed between the systems: pupils at level B in selective schools (*Sekundarschulen*) attained an average score of 63 per cent, compared with 56 per cent in the top sets in the comprehensive schools. These comparisons were based on very similar

[5]   The pre-tests in mathematics administered in primary schools at age twelve unfortunately do not cast conclusive light on the relative calibre of stream-D pupils in the two systems. As published (Rosenberg, p. 12, tables 10 and 11), it seems that the initial attainments of those pupils who went on to comprehensive schools were of slightly *higher* ability than those who went to the selective schools (published average scores, respectively, of 5.5 and 4.9, out of 19 – corresponding to 28 and 25 per cent); but there are two reasons for not accepting these average scores at face value. First, there seem to have been problems with the administration (or recording) of the pre-tests for this stream: fourteen pupils are recorded as moving to the selective *Oberschule* on the pre-test, but thirty pupils are recorded as taking the full test two years later (there is also a discrepancy – but one that is small enough to be ignored here – in the recorded numbers of pupils at the two ages in the comprehensive school, shown as 58 pupils at the pre-test and 64 at the higher age). Possibly some pupils were not tested at age twelve; or possibly (but unlikely?) there were subsequent substantial movements in the selective system from higher to lower streams. In any event, the discrepancy in pupil numbers is such that it is difficult to take the pre-test for the *Oberschule* as giving adequately reliable information for our purposes. A second reason is that even the full number of thirty pupils in the *Oberschule* represents a smaller fraction of all pupils in the selective system than the 64 pupils in the lowest stream of the comprehensive system; as above, this would lead to an expectation of higher initial average scores for the comprehensive stream. These uncertainties in total are too great to warrant any worthwhile inference.

[6]   Rosenberg (p. 26) reported identical training of teachers in the two systems and similar didactic models, but listed special AVO textbooks in her bibliography.

proportions of all pupils in the two systems (55 and 53 per cent respectively).

There is again an organisational difference which slightly muddies the waters; one of the comprehensive schools (school P) divided pupils for mathematics into four sets instead of the usual three; the top two sets both followed the same syllabus as for the comparable top selective schools, but the lower of the two sets adopted more modest targets within that syllabus. If that lower set is omitted, then the average score for the comprehensive sample rises to 64 per cent, a shade above the selective schools' average score of 63 per cent. This does not however seem a legitimate omission, since it would leave only 38 per cent of all pupils in the upper stream of the comprehensive sample compared with 55 per cent of pupils in the selective sample.

We may therefore phrase the results of the comparisons for the top group of pupils in one of two ways: we may compare either roughly the same *proportion* of top pupils in the two systems (that is 53–55 per cent of all pupils in each system), in which case we find the average score of comprehensive pupils is rather lower than of pupils in selective schools (a score of 56 compared with 63 per cent); or we may take as our standard the average *score* of 63 per cent reached by the top 55 per cent of selective school pupils, in which case we find that only 38 per cent of comprehensive pupils – a third of pupils fewer than in the selective system – were able to attain that standard.

Reasons for deterioration

The deterioration of attainments in Swiss comprehensive schools at the upper and lower ends of the range has taken place even though only very further limited changes were made: in contrast to British comprehensive schools, in Swiss comprehensive schools electronic calculators are not routinely used in mathematics lessons; a stronger emphasis in mathematics teaching remains on basic arithmetical operations; and there is no mixed-ability teaching of mathematics at secondary schools. How, then, did the deterioration take place?

An earlier Swiss study, though based on a more limited sample, offered some suggestions.[7] First, there was a third *less homework* in comprehen-

---

[7] R. Tobler, *Evaluation der Stammklassen-Niveau-Organisation 2: Leistungsaspekt am Beispiel der Mathematik* (AVO report no. 8, Zürich, 1982); esp. pp. 51 *et seq.* and 62–44.

sive schools; secondly, lessons in comprehensive schools were *interrupted* to a greater extent by socialising projects – weeks devoted to camps, outings and other special projects; thirdly, *motivation* was lower. The last was noticed especially among pupils just below the top: they regarded themselves as doing well compared with the majority who were below them in their comprehensive school, whereas their peers in selective *Sekundarschulen* felt a greater incentive to match others in their class. In relation to pupils of lower academic attainments, it was frequently mentioned on our visits to Swiss *Realschulen* that such pupils are more strongly motivated as a result of having a single form teacher for most subjects, who understands better their relative strengths and weaknesses; while in AVO comprehensive schools each pupil is taught by a greater number of teachers. Further, *Realschule* pupils particularly benefit from having their own desks in their own classroom, surrounded by familiar friends; in AVO more time is spent in moving from one classroom to another, with a fresh taking of the attendance register to check for truants, and time required for 'settling down' to work again. The *Realschule* system of a single form teacher also permits the teacher to finish a topic, even if it means overrunning the normal school timetable. It is of interest to English observers that steps to *reduce* the number of teachers involved in teaching each class in comprehensive schools ('um die Lehrerwechsel zu begrenzen') have recently been considered.[8]

Great emphasis is placed by Swiss educational researchers on the social advantages resulting from pupils of all abilities being educated in the same building, and from being able to mix with one another as a result of moving to different sets according to their attainments. These social advantages are not negligible; it needs however to be recognised that there is a cost in terms of attainments – even for that very group of pupils which it is desired to help most. Changing to a higher or lower set for mathematics obviously takes place more easily and more frequently in a comprehensive than in a selective system: while this may be an advantage for the pupil who moves and in relation to that subject, one must not discount the wider psychologically disruptive effects on those pupils who benefit from the opportunity of being in a stable environment at school.

Statistical aspects

Analyses of variance in the original Swiss report showed statistically highly significant differences according to school system for the upper ability set

[8] *Schul-Statistik*, Zürich ED, 1/1991, p. 2.

B (P<0.1%), no statistically significant difference for set C, and a moderately significant difference (P=7%) for the lowest set D. These analyses included school, class and gender as additional factors, but made no allowance for the different slices of the ability range compared; this last factor, as explained above, is an important element in assessing these comparisons. Pre-test attainments in mathematics at age twelve were not brought into their statistical analyses by the Swiss researchers; had that been done, by regarding the pre-test score as a determining variable in a regression analysis (or as part of an equivalent analysis of covariance), better – but not necessarily different – estimates might have been obtained for the average gap in attainments between the school systems as a whole, and for its three component ability sets.[9]

It is true, as the Swiss researchers emphasised, that many factors affect schooling attainments apart from those taken into account in their statistical analysis, as is shown by the large residual variation among schools within each system. Nevertheless, insofar as their analysis was concerned with the *average observed differences* in pupils' attainments in mathematics, it has to be concluded that the traditional selective system in Zürich has demonstrated a statistically significant advantage over the experimental comprehensive system.[10]

[9] Such covariance analyses have been carried out, for example, in the studies for Baden-Württemberg reported by Aurin *et al.*, *op.cit.*, pp. 350 *et seq.* Our own technical preference would be to employ multiple regression analyses to estimate the *magnitude* of the average difference in pupils' attainments, and not simply its *statistical significance* which emerges from an analysis of variance.

[10] It is a fundamental virtue of statistical analyses of this type that they enable the researcher to identify significant factors despite substantial 'background noise' generated by other factors; this point does not always seem to have been appreciated by the Swiss researchers.

Index

THE NATIONAL INSTITUTE OF ECONOMIC AND SOCIAL RESEARCH PUBLICATIONS IN PRINT

published by
THE CAMBRIDGE UNIVERSITY PRESS
(available from booksellers, or in case of difficulty from the publishers)

ECONOMIC AND SOCIAL STUDIES

OCCASIONAL PAPERS

OTHER PUBLICATIONS BY CAMBRIDGE UNIVERSITY PRESS

THE NATIONAL INSTITUTE OF
ECONOMIC AND SOCIAL RESEARCH
publishes regularly
THE NATIONAL INSTITUTE ECONOMIC REVIEW

A quarterly analysis of the general economic situation in the United Kingdom and overseas with forecasts eighteen months ahead. The last issue each year usually contains an assessment of medium-term prospects. There are also in most issues special articles on subjects of interest to academic and business economists.

Annual subscriptions, £90.00 (UK and EU) and £110.00 (rest of world), also single issues for the year, £25.00, are available direct from NIESR, 2 Dean Trench Street, Smith Square, London, SW1P 3HE.

Subscriptions at a special reduced price are available to students and teachers in the United Kingdom on application to the Secretary of the Institute.

Back numbers and reprints of issues which have gone out of stock are distributed by Wm. Dawson and Sons Ltd, Cannon House, Park Farm Road, Folkestone. Microfiche copies for the years 1961–89 are available from EP Microform Ltd, Bradford Road, East Ardsley, Wakefield, Yorks.

NATIONAL INSTITUTE OCCASIONAL PAPERS
(Available from NIESR)

No.49 *UNRESOLVED ISSUES ON THE WAY TO A SINGLE CURRENCY*
By JOHN ARROWSMITH and CHRISTOPHER TAYLOR. 1996. pp. 79.

No.50 *THE INFLUENCE OF FINANCIAL INTERMEDIARIES ON THE BEHAVIOUR OF THE UK ECONOMY*
BY GARRY YOUNG. 1996. PP. 112.

Published by
SAGE PUBLICATIONS LTD
(Available from Sage and from booksellers)

ECONOMIC CONVERGENCE AND MONETARY UNION IN EUROPE. Edited by RAY BARRELL. 1992. pp. 288.
ACHIEVING MONETARY UNION IN EUROPE. By ANDREW BRITTON and DAVID MAYES. 1992. pp. 160.
MACROECONOMIC POLICY COORDINATION IN EUROPE: THE ERM AND MONETARY UNION. Edited by RAY BARRELL and JOHN D. WHITLEY. 1993. pp. 294.